BUSINESS TRANSFORMATION

Other publications by Van Haren Publishing

Van Haren Publishing (VHP) specializes in titles on Best Practices, methods and standards within four domains:
- IT and IT Management
- Architecture (Enterprise and IT)
- Business Management and
- Project Management

Van Haren Publishing offers a wide collection of whitepapers, templates, free e-books, trainer materials etc. in the **Van Haren Publishing Knowledge Base**: www.vanharen.net for more details.

Van Haren Publishing is also publishing on behalf of leading organizations and companies: ASLBiSL Foundation, BRMI, CA, Centre Henri Tudor, Gaming Works, IACCM, IAOP, Innovation Value Institute, IPMA-NL, ITSqc, NAF, Ngi/NGN, PMI-NL, PON, The Open Group, The SOX Institute.

Topics are (per domain):

IT and IT Management	Architecture (Enterprise and IT)	Project, Program and Risk Management
ABC of ICT	ArchiMate®	A4-Projectmanagement
ASL®	GEA®	DSDM/Atern
CATS CM®	Novius Architectuur Methode	ICB / NCB
CMMI®	TOGAF®	ISO 21500
COBIT®		MINCE®
e-CF	**Business Management**	M_o_R®
ISO 20000	BABOK® Guide	MSP™
ISO 27001/27002	BiSL®	P3O®
ISPL	BRMBOK™	PMBOK® Guide
IT-CMF™	BTF	PRINCE2®
IT Service CMM	EFQM	
ITIL®	eSCM	
MOF	IACCM	
MSF	ISA-95	
SABSA	ISO 9000/9001	
	OPBOK	
	SAP	
	SixSigma	
	SOX	
	SqEME®	

For the latest information on VHP publications, visit our website: www.vanharen.net.

Business Transformation Framework

To get from Strategy to Execution

BTF version 2016

Jeroen Stoop

Sjoerd Staffhorst

Remco Bekker

Tjerk Hobma

Colophon

Title:	Business Transformation Framework – To get from Strategy to Execution
Subtitle:	BTF version 2016
Authors:	Jeroen Stoop Sjoerd Staffhorst Remco Bekker Tjerk Hobma
Text edit:	Steve Newton
Publisher:	Van Haren Publishing, Zaltbommel, www.vanharen.net
ISBN Hard copy:	978 94 018 0026 6
ISBN eBook:	978 94 018 0580 3
Edition:	First edition, first impression, March 2016
Lay out and DTP:	CO2 Premedia, Amersfoort – NL
Copyright:	© Van Haren Publishing, 2014, 2016

Acknowledgments

We would like to thank all people whose support and contributions enabled us to write this book.

Of course, first of all we must thank Marc Beijen, Eric Broos and Etienne Lucas. Their earlier books paved the way for the business transformation planning approach that is presented in this book.

We also offer many thanks to our colleague Marloes Smit and former colleague Peter Verboort for their contributions to various chapters of this book. We would also like to thank Raimond Brookman from Info Support for his help in working out the IT Infrastructure & Facilities aspect. Many other colleagues also took the time and trouble to read the draft version of this book and provide useful, critical and above all constructive feedback, for which we are very grateful.

A special thanks goes out to Stefan Stroosnijder who supported us with the translation from the Dutch to this English version.

Finally, we thank Bart Verbrugge, our publisher, who kept close tabs on us in terms of content, consistency, readability and relationships with other methods and frameworks.

February 2016
The authors

Foreword

In my opinion, the authors have succeeded once again in creating an excellent combination of theory and practice in this latest edition of their book on business transformation planning. It is a highly readable book. I am a practical person. I have no need for management books with high-flown theories, but I do like practical tips. This book gives you everything you need to start working with the Business Transformation Framework. It describes how to translate the changes needed in an organization from the strategy into the organizational design of the future, and how you can apply this to your own organizational design. The impact that this has and the required actions come together in the project portfolio.

The first few chapters are more general in nature. These in-depth chapters give you some firm guidance on the Business Transformation Framework. With this knowledge, you can start plotting out your own framework. The Business Transformation Model, as a central part of the framework, provides you with a basic guidance and structure, so you get a holistic overview and see all the interconnections. This book makes numerous references to existing literature and popular theories and models. It draws ample connections to these, which links up excellently with a manager's knowledge.

This book presents a sound method. Business transformation planning is about more than just 'changing the business'. This book also focuses on change activities for 'running an organization'. It is precisely this combination that makes the Business Transformation Framework so powerful and this book provides excellent examples of how to use it.

I have a great deal of experience with the Business Transformation Framework at Delta Lloyd. In my experience this framework significantly increases the likelihood of lasting change. It has helped me to:
- Combine change activities in the run & change organizations and merge them into a single plan.
- Create the optimal project portfolio with limited budgets and resources.
- Provide senior management with support in prioritization and decision-making and then explain this to the rest of the organization.

The integral approach and the required cooperation during setup make a major contribution to this. It's about more than just changing the processes, or just the strategy, or just IT. It's all about the interrelationships and dependencies. Drawing up a business transformation plan provides much more added-value than just the product: the business transformation portfolio. You must implement changes together with employees, and it's certainly beneficial if you start with an approach that is recognizable to both management and staff. By developing the approach together, it will be shared, felt and implemented throughout the organization. In my view, that is the added-value of this method.

One point of attention is that business transformation planning is too often viewed as a one-time or annual exercise. That is not a desirable situation: it is a continuous process. You are changing constantly, so you also need to keep pace with these changes. In addition, drawing up a business transformation plan is not an end in itself: it is a tool. The Business Transformation Framework supports the structured and integral translation of strategy into a project portfolio. You should also dissuade people from skipping ahead to drawing up the project calendar, because you would miss out on the added-value of the preceding steps. The connection between business and IT is particularly important.

Every IT manager should be familiar with this book. It offers an excellent account of linking business up with IT and making the right choices. IT managers should take the initiative in introducing the use of these methods.

In addition, this book is also of interest to managers. After all, every manager deals with change. In my opinion, there is no longer any such thing as a company that is free from change. Moreover, this framework also helps you communicate with employees at all levels of the organization on changes and associated activities. A highly useful tool!

Carola Wijkamp – Hermsen
Director of General Personal Insurance
Delta Lloyd Group
January 2016

Contents

Introduction

0.1   About this book

This book is the official description of the Business Transformation Framework, acronym: BTF. The Business Transformation Framework replaces the previous framework described in the Dutch-language book *"Business-informatieplanning"* (Beijen, 2003). The ability to combine business planning and information planning is essential to any organization that hopes to stay ahead of the game in today's fast-paced world. The Business Transformation Framework consists of the Business Transformation Model as the central part, but also includes an approach for business transformation planning. Despite the difference between a Framework and a Model, we will refer to both with the acronym BTF.

The BTF provides the foundation and tools to draw up a business transformation plan. The BTF has been in development for over 20 years now, and has grown into a methodical and proven approach. The full potential of the BTF can only truly be fully realized when it is regarded as a way of thinking and acting. This becomes very clear when an organization (as a whole) has developed the ability to quickly make the translation, whenever needed, from "What do we want to achieve?" or "What is happening to us?" to "What specifically should we do about it tomorrow?", thus seamlessly laying the connections between the different aspects of running an organization as well as between departments and employees. By 'aspects of running an organization', we mean:
• Customers & Services;
• Processes & Organization;
• Information & Applications;
• IT Infrastructure & Facilities.

The good news is that the BTF, as a way of thinking and acting, can be developed and learned, including in your own organization!

Oddly enough, the BTF was not originally developed for use in organizational changes, but rather as a restorative approach in the implementation of information planning. Gradually however, a broader application arose for organizational changes, resulting in its development from the original 'BTF' framework to the current BTF. We can see the same development that resulted in the BTF in various trends in the market, as described quite elegantly in the book *Business/IT Fusion* (Hinssen, 2011). In practice, we have also noticed it becoming increasingly difficult to separate change in IT from change in business. The degree to which IT has been integrated into internal processes and even into the provision of services in organizations now requires an integral approach that brings together business and IT. The BTF offers that approach.

One striking example here is a practical case in which the BTF was used in a stalled merger process between four organizations. The collective information plan never got off the ground and was bogged down in all kinds of expressions of resistance. Within just five weeks, the BTF was used to create a business transformation plan with representation from each of the merger parties and under the sponsorship of the Director of Operations. Where needed, this process took into consideration a much broader scope than just information systems and IT infrastructure. Nowadays, it simply is not possible to have four merger parties use the same application landscape without also examining issues such as processes, organization, product structure and services. Making choices here also requires another marketing plan, policy, a vision for organizational control, etc. Thus, the plan clearly showed that in order to achieve the defined goals, it would take a lot more than just IT applications. The extremely fast-paced multidisciplinary, participative and fixed-term approach left practically no resistance to speak of. The collaboration was pleasant, if somewhat uncomfortable, but always constructive. After the presentation of the plan to the three directors, the CEO remarked: "So, in that case, this will be our transformation plan for the next three years!"

Table 0.1   The three orders of organizational change (Bartunek & Koch, 1987)

Order of change	Description
1st-order change Adjust (or improve) existing situation	"The current situation is known, the problems have been identified, and the solutions are clear. This is a change from a known situation to a new, target situation. It is also clear what we need to do to achieve the change. The customers, products and markets remain stable. It is about serving current customers better and cheaper with existing products. The strategy, structure and culture also remain the same. What *does* change is technical systems and work routines."
2nd-order change Modernize the current situation	"The second level focuses on modernizing the current situation. The current situation is more or less known, but the new situation is not yet entirely clear. Some key questions are: What will the new situation look like, and how can we get from the current situation to the new one? This 'second-order change' is about modernization of internal processes and customer relations. This means a change in strategy, structure, culture and technology. People's working methodologies and behaviors in the organization are also part of the change. This may involve: • A merger or partnership between companies; • Introduction of a new product; • A new form of service, for which existing departments have to collaborate in a different way; • A reorganization of internal processes. 'Second-order changes' are more involved than 'first-order changes'. One characteristic feature is that the strategy, structure, technology and processes are changed in a cohesive manner. These kinds of change processes also benefit from a phased and carefully considered approach involving all of the stakeholders."
3rd-order change	"A 'third-order change' is a transformation[1], i.e. seeking out new possibilities in a situation of uncertainty. In reality, everything is subject to change. The identity of the organization is under pressure and uncertainty arises surrounding its *raison d'être*. The current situation is unclear and the future is also uncertain. The changes are far-reaching and affect everyone involved. Transformative changes take guts and leadership."

---

1   In the Business Transformation Framework and therefore in this book, the word 'transformation' not only refers to 3rd-order changes, but to the whole of 1st-, 2nd- and 3rd-order changes needed to implement the strategy

We are placing the BTF within the large field of change management, and that calls for more precise positioning. For this, we use the typology of the various orders of organizational change described above. Table 0.1 gives a summary of these.

The BTF plays an especially prominent role in changes of the first and second orders. For third-order changes, the BTF may be applied as one of a broad range of actions necessary in such cases. Third-order changes often come hand-in-hand with a large number of changes of the first and second order. Such changes require highly experienced change management specialists with excellent change management skills and knowledge of, and experience in, a variety of interventions.

However, you do not bring about change simply by planning. There is a great deal more to it than that. The Novius Business Empowerment Framework shows the different disciplines

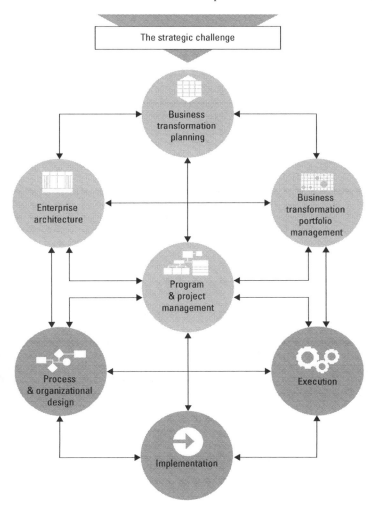

Figure 0.1 The Novius Business Empowerment Framework

that are also required. See figure 0.1. This also positions the BTF directly in relation to other methods in areas such as enterprise and IT architecture, project management, program management, process & organizational design and implementation. Appendix 1 provides a diagram of the interrelationships between the different Novius frameworks.

As you can see from the Novius Business Empowerment Framework, the BTF is used to develop a business transformation portfolio. Changes (of the first and second orders) are largely brought about in the form of programs and projects. Programs and projects yield results that need to be implemented in the organization. In this process, the content of the change is controlled by enterprise architecture and the planning by portfolio management. Table 0.2 gives a number of examples of commonly used methods and techniques for the other disciplines in the Novius Business Empowerment Framework.

Table 0.2   Examples of commonly used management methods and frameworks linking up with the disciplines in the Novius Business Empowerment Framework

Discipline	Examples of methods and techniques
Enterprise architecture	Novius Architecture Method, TOGAF/ArchiMate, DYA
Portfolio management	MoP® (Management of Portfolios)
Program and project management	PRINCE2, PMBOK Guide, IPMA's ICB, MSP
Process & organizational design	BPMN, UML
Realization	Agile, Scrum

In many instances the BTF affects the entire organization. This means there are frequently numerous stakeholders involved in the application of this framework. This book is primarily geared towards people directly involved in the execution of the BTF or in the decision-making for project prioritization, allocation of resources, etc. Some examples here would be business, IT and other managers, advisors, program & project managers and change managers. Thus, this book is intended for a broad audience.

The topic of business transformation planning, and thus also the BTF, is quite extensive. In order to explain the framework properly in this book, we opted for an approach that is as intuitive as possible. Chapter 1 covers why the BTF has proven to be a highly useful tool in the design, planning, development and control of organizational change. It also introduces the structure of the rest of the book. Chapters 2 and 3 discuss change design and planning. Chapter 2 goes into detail on the steps needed to turn a strategy into a business transformation portfolio. Chapter 3 focuses on the most involved step: cohesive analysis and design of Customers & Services, Processes & Organization, Information & Applications and IT Infrastructure & Facilities. Chapter 4 covers the process of creating a business transformation plan. This is not a complete 'change management' handbook, but it does tell you – based on twenty years of practical experience – what approach and working methodologies have proven effective. Chapter 5 does not discuss the creation of the business transformation plan any further, but rather looks at how to effectively control the change. Finally, chapter 6 gives you the necessary guidance to begin working with the BTF.

0.2 BTF - Business Transformation Framework

Does the BTF have anything more to add to everything that has already been written about planning for organizational change? Many who pick up this book will undoubtedly ask themselves this question. The answer is: Yes. After all, the BTF is a highly practical framework that supports the design, development, planning and control of organizational change. Simply put: the BTF gives you a firm grip on organizational change!

An information plan is not the same thing as a transformation plan. The similarities are in fact rather significant and the evolution of the previous version of the 'BTF' Framework from 2003 to the current BTF is also highly understandable, especially in retrospect.

The starting point for both cases is the strategy of the organization. Based on this, any constraints and opportunities for improvement can be identified in the *current situation* and a design can be prepared for the *target situation*. Resolution of constraints, taking up opportunities for improvement and implementation of the target situation require an organizational change, typically achieved by means of programs and projects. For drafting both an information plan and a business transformation plan, we examine all aspects of running an organization: Customers & Services, Processes & Organization, Information & Applications and IT Infrastructure & Facilities. The difference here is that an information plan is normally based on choices already made in the areas of Customers & Services and Processes & Organization. In information planning, this is often referred to as 'business'. In contrast, when making a business transformation plan, integral choices are made with regard to changes in all aspects of running an organization. The scope of the design for the change is thus much broader.

A major difference between an information plan and a business transformation plan arises during creation of the plan. A business transformation plan involves more stakeholders and higher stakes. This is certainly the case if the organizational design and governance is part of the scope. This requires a great deal more in the way of change management skills from the business transformation planner(s). The business transformation portfolio also contains many other interventions, which in an information plan are mostly preliminary studies and implementation projects. Some examples here would be training programs, organizational changes, etc.

The BTF has evolved into a methodical approach highly geared towards integral process & organizational design. Just as with the gradual shift from pure information planning to integral business transformation planning, additional emphasis is now being placed on the development of the business transformation plan. This concerns aspects such as the process, control, working methodologies, project organization and other stakeholders. We have actually gone through the normal stages in that regard, from consciously incompetent to consciously (increasingly) competent. At this time, our point of view is that the development of the business transformation plan is at least as important as the design of the transformation. Development and design go hand-in-hand because making a business transformation plan is the first step in this transformation! See figure 0.2.

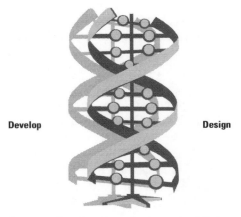

Develop   **Design**

Figure 0.2   Transformation is development and design

Design mainly concerns making design decisions. The emphasis lies in a systematic analysis and a future description of the organization and its information processes. This ensures insight, a holistic overview and quality. So, from time immemorial, design has been geared more towards the 'hard' side.

Development involves getting a business transformation process underway and shaping change so that people in the organization make effective and enthusiastic contributions to the results to be achieved. This firmly embeds the new objectives. Development is mainly geared towards the softer side of change – the human side. Design and development influence one another in the implementation of business transformations. The right combination results in the best solutions with a strong base of support.

We should add a brief comment here. This is because we need to be clear on one thing: a successful organizational change often does in fact require more than just the BTF. This is because the framework doesn't address all possible issues that may impede a transformation. Some examples here would be the need for leadership development, having to repair disrupted relationships, the prevention of resistance due to negative experiences in the past, the natural human tendency to fear change, the existence of unhealthy political relationships and conflicting self-interests, etc. These kinds of situations require change managers with extensive experience and mastery of a broad range of interventions. However, the BTF can also offer a great deal of added-value in these cases, as one of the key tools applied by change managers to shape the transformation.

1 The BTF is an excellent tool for organizational change

The most successful organizations are those that are able to translate their strategy into an operational implementation and, in doing so, are also able to keep pace with the numerous developments in the environment. Standing still is not an option. Every day the latest demands and expectations coming from outside of the organization must be met and its *raison d'être* be proved again. Citizens, customers, clients and patients are becoming increasingly critical and articulate. Competitive relationships between organizations are in constant flux and more and more organizations are dealing with an international market instead of a local market. New or changing national and international laws and regulations require adjustments in the organization. These are all examples of a changing environment to which the organization must anticipate and react. The list of possible changes is long, because in addition to political, social and economic developments, we also have technological advances arising at an ever-increasing pace. (See also figure 1.1.) This means that organizations must anticipate their constantly changing environment and also identify additional possibilities and opportunities for growth and improvement.

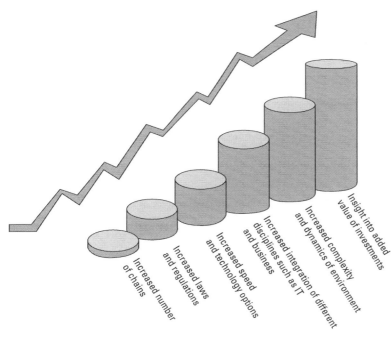

Figure 1.1 The continuously changing environment in which organizations are operating offers possibilities and opportunities for growth and improvement

In addition to the aforementioned external factors, there are also internal drivers that make organizations feel compelled to change. After all, an organization is a collaborative relationship between people based around a specific objective or mission. These people will also put demands on, and have expectations of, the organization. A case in point is the influx of a new generation of employees who find it normal to work in a manner independent of time, place and device. However, a healthy drive to achieve ambitions will also result in a continuous stream of suggestions for improvement and, sometimes, radically innovative ideas. It does not matter whether an organization opts for minimal costs, the most innovative product, or the best solution for the customer. Organizations will always strive towards perfection, in order to remain attractive to their customers and distinguish themselves from the competition. Ambition also ensures that organizations will change.

The above is not new. You cannot read any book, article or blog nowadays without hearing impassioned speeches warning that organizational change is coming to us with increasing frequency, speed and complexity. You could fill not only shelves but entire libraries with publications on this topic. There is plenty of reading material for any interested party. So as not to labor the point, it will suffice to conclude that change indeed should not be an end in itself, but that modernization is in fact vital to organizations and that organizational change has certainly not become any simpler in recent years.

Organizational change is therefore difficult. This book provides a framework to help you take on this challenge. Based on the BTF (see figure 1.2), we will explain how you can make the connection between strategy and business transformation portfolio within an organization and how to create a business transformation portfolio that is used to actually achieve the intended effects of the change.

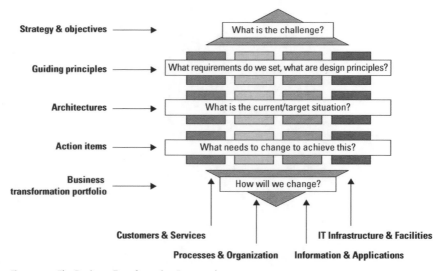

Figure 1.2   The Business Transformation Framework

Despite the enormous amount of attention given to organizational change in recent years, the reality is that there has been resistance to such change. We regularly see statistics for the success rates of projects and business transformation initiatives. It does not matter so much whether the success rate is 50% or 70%, or when an organizational change is, or is not, deemed successful. These kinds of success rates are in fact too low and do not exactly inspire confidence that organizations are able to implement change successfully with a reasonable degree of certainty. That is precisely the hard part. After over twenty years of practical experience with the BTF, we firmly believe that preparing, planning and controlling an organizational change with this approach increases its success rate enormously. Proper preparation is half the battle. We can cite several reasons why the BTF can be a useful tool for organizational change.

1.1   The BTF has proven itself in practice

The development of the BTF was based on practical experience, on what was and was not working. Therefore, it is not primarily a theoretical model or theory, although a significant portion draws upon existing theories and we make ample use of existing models. It is above all a best practice approach, i.e. based on a wealth of practical experience.

The BTF was developed based on several tools for successful execution of information planning within organizations. In the early 1990s, Novius introduced these tools with the objective, among other things, of bringing the planning for information systems and IT infrastructure to the attention of senior management. For this, it was necessary to draw up plans that would be supported and understood by the directors – plans that would make the complexity of the IT world comprehensible to directors through the use of visualizations and by demonstrating the interrelationships between business and IT.

Currently, in the majority of organizations, automated information systems are an integral part of running an organization. This means organizational changes practically always have an IT component. The reverse is also true: IT initiatives almost always have an impact on other aspects of running a business. There is a strong desire for integrated planning across all aspects of operational management. This change in thinking has also had repercussions for the BTF and the approach to its implementation. The BTF has evolved over the course of time from an approach to information planning to a practical method for the design, development, planning and control that is integral to organizational change.

Getting a better grip on organizational change starts with organization-wide, structured planning and control of the business transformation. Experience has shown that successful change (incidentally, just like the successful implementation of the desired information systems and IT infrastructure) largely depends on cohesion as well as collaboration. This is because organizational change does not occur all by itself, in some separate state of isolation, until completion. In many unsuccessful or partially unsuccessful organizational changes, it is apparent that adequate cohesion was lacking between the business strategy and the business transformation portfolio, or between the different aspects of running an organization and that collaboration was lacking at various levels in the organization.

Organizations will only change if the people in those organizations are actually willing *and* able to change, *and* then actually do so. Experience has taught us that change must always be viewed and applied cohesively and collaboratively. In practice, the BTF has proven to be an excellent tool for getting a better handle on change, in no small part because it introduces cohesion and promotes collaboration.

1.2   The BTF helps translate the strategy into specific action

Organizational change includes activities at all levels: from the strategic choices made by management to a different way of thinking and acting in the workplace. It is necessary to tie these two ends together in order to achieve successful organizational change.

The change must be outlined based on the strategy so that it has a clear direction. Changes take direction from the mission, vision and objectives that the organization has set for itself. The BTF ensures a vision-driven business transformation by translating the strategy into activities that must be performed in order to achieve the strategy. However, a concrete strategy and clear objectives cannot be translated directly into a business transformation portfolio. The complexity of organizations themselves and the complexity of their environments are simply too great for this. The BTF helps bridge the gap between strategy and implementation, by ensuring a structured translation of the strategy into a business transformation portfolio. See Figure 1.3.

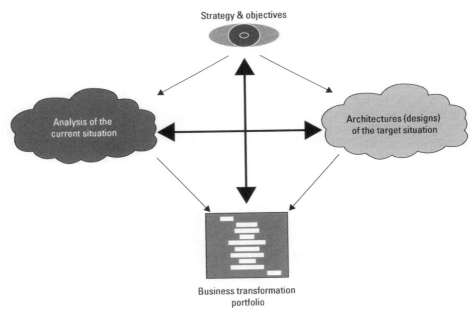

Figure 1.3   From strategy & objectives to a business transformation portfolio

The BTF is highly action-oriented: all of the activities in the approach are ultimately intended to provide a collection of action items that will be clustered into programs, projects and change activities in the line organization and that must be performed in order to implement the desired changes. The general term 'organizational change' is used to cover the programs, projects, interventions and activities to be implemented in the line organization. Chapter 2 goes into further detail on this.

1.3   The BTF makes cohesion in organizations manageable

In addition to cohesion between strategy and implementation, cohesion is also always necessary between all of the aspects concerned with running an organization. For successful organizational change, it is necessary to link up and harmonize different aspects of the organization. Integral change is certainly <u>not</u> achieved by having marketeers brainstorming new products in isolation, process specialists working in isolation to decide how to optimize processes, HR staff headhunting in isolation, IT staff designing new systems in isolation, general services arranging accommodations in isolation, etc.

Harmonization between the different aspects of running an organization, and thus also between different departments and employees, is necessary, among other reasons, in order to prevent the organization from creating customer expectations (such as delivery within 24 hours) that it can never meet because the internal processes are not set up for it. Another key harmonization issue is the method for providing optimal IT support to the processes. The BTF brings together the different capabilities in an organization and ensures more mutual consultation. After all, the organization must be able to produce its new product. A minor change in the internal process can have a major impact on the supporting systems. Understanding this is a key result of performing business transformation planning, but understanding alone is not enough for an organizational change to succeed. Figure 1.4 shows how the different aspects of running a business (Customers & Services, Processes & Organization, Information & Applications and IT Infrastructure & Facilities) influence one another.

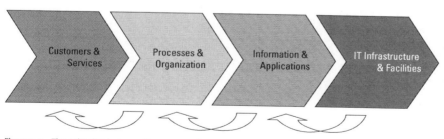

Figure 1.4   The cohesion between the aspects of running a business

Chapter 3 examines how it all works together when it comes to applying cohesion and harmonization between the different aspects of running an organization.

1.4   The BTF expressly takes the current situation into consideration

Successful organizational change requires linking the desired target situation up with the current situation. It is important to realize that a business transformation plan is not typically developed in perfect isolation. Planned changes must be analyzed in relation to the current situation. Constraints from practical experience must be included as part of the transformation activity. Issues to be resolved in order to achieve the target situation must be addressed. It is also vital to be realistic here, so a feasible and desirable path is developed to get from the current situation to the target situation. Of course, keep in mind that there are many paths up the mountain.

The BTF achieves cohesion between the desired change and the current situation by incorporating the bottlenecks and opportunities for improvement from the current situation into the transformation design phase. In addition, the plan works with 'architectures' from both the current and target situations, to provide the picture of the contents of the change that is necessary to achieve the set goals. This picture can then be used to derive the specific actions that are needed to implement the change. Chapters 2 and 3 discuss this in further detail and provide the basic guidance you will need to start working with the BTF.

1.5   The BTF promotes collaboration and creates a base of support

Experience has shown that organizations can only change if the people in the organization really want to change, and actually act to do so. You must be willing and able to change, and you must actually do it. This means that the change process deserves a great deal of attention. And that starts from day one, with planning the change. This means that the interventions must be geared towards participation, communication, involvement, providing ownership, support, transfer of knowledge, skills and culture and learning. Collaboration (in all of its various forms) is critical in this:

1. Collaboration is geared towards involvement of those employees in an organization who must implement the change. Support for the desired change by these employees is crucial. It is not enough for the change to be worked out on paper. All stakeholder employees must support and carry out the change.
2. Collaboration is an effective way to bridge the gap between thought and action. Management and employees in the workplace work together in this process to design and plan the desired changes. This process ensures that management's planning is firmly based on reality and feasibility and encourages ideas from the shop floor.
3. Collaboration contributes to a cohesive understanding of what is required in order to implement the changes. Employees from various disciplines in the organization work together, such as staff from Finance, IT, Marketing, etc. This ensures optimal use of

specialist knowledge and the full range of diverse ideas. By doing so, the changes are designed and planned in an 'integral' manner, i.e. taking into account the interrelationships between the various disciplines in the organization.

The BTF offers a structured approach so people and organizations can transform themselves. Chapter 4 goes into detail on how this works in practice.

1.6 The BTF helps stay on course during business transformations

Due to all of the attention given to organizational change, we sometimes seem to forget that organizations must continue to perform normally from day-to-day. It is not just about 'changing the business': it is really about 'running an organization'. This means changing 'with the store open'. This does not make things any easier, and it requires a lot of organizational capability. The challenge is to keep the organizational change on course whilst also dealing with the range of external and internal influences. See Figure 1.5.

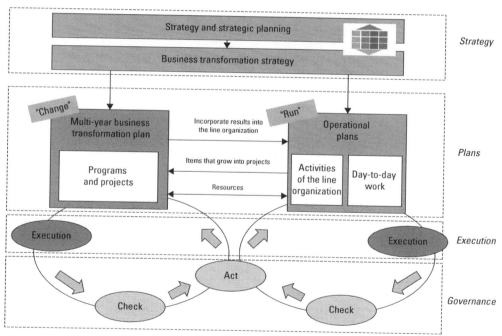

Figure 1.5 Interrelationships between 'run the organization' and 'change the organization'

Therefore, there is a relationship between business transformation and running an organization from day-to-day. The available expertise, resources and finances must be shared: people are busy with both the day-to-day state of affairs and the transformation, and they require funds for both. The available assets required to implement the business transformation portfolio are limited by the ambitions of the organization, and especially by the requirements of day-to-day operations. In many organizations, the vast majority of available resource is consumed by maintaining day-to-day operations ('running an organization') and is therefore not allocated to business transformations.

The feasibility of the business transformation portfolio and thus also of the overall organizational change may come under strain from changes in the assets that are required and available. This means that careful monitoring of the availability and utilization of human resources and business assets is vital. The BTF ensures that you stay on course during the implementation of the business transformation portfolio in terms of both the timescales and budget by means of a properly designed portfolio management process.

In addition to implementing the business transformation portfolio within time and budget, it is also critical to maintain control over content. During execution of the planned organizational change, market conditions may change, alternative solutions may arise and internal outlooks on the future may vary. In addition to this, running a business involves continuous improvement and adjustments, thereby creating a risk that the implemented situation will increasingly diverge from the target situation. Implementing the BTF requires a great deal of attention on control over content and quality, and the business transformation plan provides the footing for this. The goal is not to adhere to a pre-defined course regardless of the costs, but rather to make well thought through decisions. This can be guaranteed in the implementation by using an architecture which ensures adherence to content in the implementation of the business transformation portfolio. Chapter 5 covers this in further detail.

1.7   The BTF can be used for numerous issues

You may have the impression that the BTF is primarily geared towards drafting multi-year change planning which is implemented after a significant strategy change, an external event with major impact or serious internal structural issues. The BTF is indeed excellently suited to these situations. However, the BTF can in fact also be used to operationalize new strategies, merge organizations and implement new laws and regulations requiring the reorganization of entire divisions and business models. In addition, it is used in situations that call for 'getting the house in order' in the first instance or require a situation to be stabilized. These are some of the main reasons why people typically consider the BTF. However, it is usually only those organizations with specific experience in this approach that are able to exploit its full potential.

Aside from these specific applications, the BTF is more of a way of thinking and acting, which can provide lasting support for organizational change processes. This becomes clear when an organization (as a whole) has developed the ability to quickly make the translation, when required, from "What do we want to achieve?" or "What is happening to us?" to "What specifically should we do about it tomorrow?", thus seamlessly laying the connections between the different aspects of running an organization and between departments and employees. This ability is not only useful for extensive transformations, but also for tasks such as defining programs or projects and conducting an impact analysis.

This same ability also works in reverse: how can we get a quick answer to the question of whether or not all of our transformation efforts will actually produce the desired target situation? In other words: to make the translation from "What are we all actually doing here?" and "Are we actually getting where we want to go?" to the specific, practical measures needed to adjust the situation. One example here would be an audit on a change program or project.

You may also have the impression that the entire BTF activity takes at least a month to complete. In fact, it can range from a few weeks to, occasionally, a few months, though this latter case may well be an organization's first experience with the BTF. The same approach may however be applied over half a day, but that requires a certain level of experience. Of course, this does not produce the same results in terms of depth and completeness, but depending on the management requirements, it may be all that is required. Sometimes an initial indicative scan is enough, such as to find out what new legal rules and regulations mean for the organization (an impact assessment).

In a business unit dealing with planning and operation at a large semi-public organization in the transportation sector, numerous factors are at play. These factors can be almost anything: internal ambitions or major constraints, externally imposed public tasks, new legislation, etc. Decision-making is difficult because these issues have not been worked through in sufficient detail. Then some problems arise. Firstly, there is linguistic confusion over the various issues since all stakeholders have developed their own definitions which means, in turn, that they also have their own assumptions, values and desires. On top of this, the issues have not been worked through in adequate detail in order to determine their impact on the various options available.

In this case a workshop is held on a single evening to consider all of the issues, using the BTF. Out of this ten micro business transformation plans are created. It is decided to use an interview technique in which a workshop participant interviews another participant and goes through an actual business transformation process in 30 to 60 minutes. This approach provides adequate insight into, and an appropriate holistic overview of, the different issues in order to address any points of uncertainty, greatly clarify understanding of the significance of the issues and plan the subsequent steps.

The following chapters will largely describe the BTF in the context of somewhat more extensive, one-time organizational changes. However, we challenge the reader to consider the wider application to the method based on the thinking and working described in this book.

1.8   Summary

The BTF is a framework for the development, design, planning and control of organizational change. The BTF is based on a best practice approach. The BTF helps translate strategy into a specific business transformation portfolio and ensure consistency between the following aspects: Customers & Services, Processes & Organization, Information & Applications and IT Infrastructure & Facilities. The BTF is a key tool in this. In addition to the development of a target situation, the BTF expressly takes into account constraints and opportunities in the current situation. A multidisciplinary approach, involving numerous people from the organization, ensures a higher-quality plan and a broader base of support. A well-developed plan with justified choices helps you stay on course during the transformation. The BTF is a way of thinking *and* acting. That is why it is suitable for a variety of organizational issues related to change. Sometimes, this requires an extensive, long-term project, but on other occasions needs no more than a workshop lasting a couple of hours.

2 From strategy to a specific business transformation plan – a step-by-step approach

In many organizations, once a year the management holds discussions on what projects should be undertaken during the coming year and what resources need to be made available for them. This is often a difficult discussion. Not only are there typically more resources needed than are, or can be, made available, it is also very difficult to determine which projects should be prioritized over others. This makes it hard to tell if:

- The planned strategy will work;
- The set goals will actually be achieved;
- Cohesive design choices have been made;
- The necessary changes have been mapped-out in full;
- The interrelationships between projects are properly understood and manageable.

This creates a high risk that scarce people and resources will not be allocated to those projects with the most added-value for the organization.

Making a mental leap from strategy to a specific business transformation portfolio is simply too difficult. The dynamics and dependencies in today's organizations are too numerous and the interrelationships between the design choices are too complex. Therefore, translating the strategy into a cohesive business transformation portfolio requires a structured and gradual approach.

The BTF offers this structured and gradual approach and has proven itself in practice as an excellent tool for the design, planning and control of organizational improvements in a structured manner throughout the organization. On the one hand, the BTF helps with the continuous alignment of strategy and objectives in the business transformation portfolio. On the other hand, it helps make cohesive design choices with regard to the different aspects of running an organization in order to analyze constraints and opportunities for improvement in a cohesive manner.

The BTF is arranged along two dimensions. On the vertical axis, the business transformation portfolio and the strategy are plotted on a single line, and the horizontal axis gives the alignment between the different aspects of running a business. See figure 2.1. This chapter explains the vertical dimension and goes into detail about how to use the BTF to apply cohesion between strategy and the business transformation portfolio. Going through the framework horizontally, i.e. cohesive analysis and design of the different aspects of running an organization, is covered in detail in chapter 3.

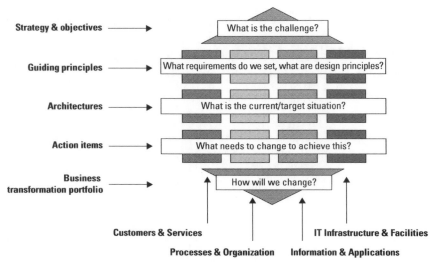

Figure 2.1   The Business Transformation Framework

The BTF helps bridge the gap between strategy and implementation by 'guiding' translation of the strategy into a business transformation portfolio in several steps. See Figure 2.2.

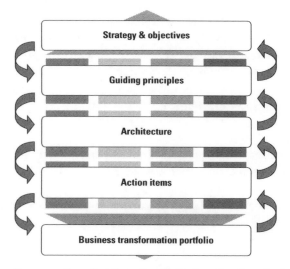

Figure 2.2   The vertical dimension of the Business Transformation Framework: strategy & objectives must be cohesive both from the top down and the bottom up

The first step starts at the top of the framework with defining the strategy and objectives. A good strategy is vital to defining the changes. Good strategies must be specific enough and provide adequate direction, in order to provide the foundation for the business transformation. Incidentally, this book does not cover the differences between successful and less successful strategies. For this, we refer you to the large volume of literature specifically on this topic, such as Kaplan & Norton (1993, 2004), Porter (1998), Kim & Mauborgne

(2004), Mintzberg (2008), Johnson, Scholes & Whittington (2008) and Hamel & Prahalad (1996). Section 2.1 discusses an approach for fine-tuning and elaborating the strategy of an organization, which provides an adequate foundation for translation into a business transformation portfolio.

Step 2 is the formulation of guiding principles. These provide direction when making design choices for the organization. Section 2.2 explains the guiding principles and how to derive them from the strategy.

Step 3 is to analyze the current situation and outline the target situation. Enterprise architecture is used for this. This is outlined in general terms in section 2.3, and covered in further detail in chapter 3.

Step 4 formulates the action items based on a comparison between the current and target situations. Section 2.4 explains how this works in practice.

Finally, Step 5 translates the action items into a business transformation portfolio. Section 2.5 details this process.

Although this chapter describes the BTF from the top-down, cohesion must also be thoroughly ensured from the bottom-up. All programs, projects and activities of the line organization must collectively include all action items needed to implement the transformation from the current situation to the target situation. In this process, the target situation must meet the selected guiding principles. It should always be possible to clearly associate the organizational improvement elaborated in this process in terms of content and planning with the execution of the strategy and the objectives.

2.1 Elaborating the strategy and the objectives as a foundation for the planned business transformation

A specific strategy is needed in order to outline the desired design for an organization and identify the changes it requires. By strategy, we mean the entirety of the mission, vision and core values, up to and including specific objectives. With a clear strategy, an organization can define its ambitions over the long term. An organization uses its strategy to guide the allocation of people and resources in order to ensure that its objectives are actually achieved. The strategy also provides a picture of the desired direction and target situation, which is necessary for a targeted transformation. The clearer and more specific the strategy and objectives, the easier it will be to define the required organizational design and plan business transformation activities.

Successful organizations focus intently on their strategy. Unfortunately, in practice, most strategies turn out to be too vague, lacking in direction, unknown to management and staff and sometimes even non-existent. At the beginning of a BTF project it is a good idea to draw up an inventory of what is available in terms of strategy and how complete and specific it is.

The strategy invariably includes a breakdown with the organization's primary objectives at the top and SMART objectives for the planning period at the bottom. Higher goals are often referred to as the 'mission, core values and vision'. However, other terms are sometimes used as well, such as: 'audacious goals', 'Big Hairy Audacious Goals', BHAGs (Collins & Porras, 1994) or 'strategic intent' (Hamel & Prahalad, 1996).

Using several intermediate steps, the objectives for the planning period are derived from the top objective. In general, the intermediate steps are:
• Formulation of a strategic agenda or strategic goals;
• A description or illustration of the business model;
• An elaboration of the strategy.

Figure 2.3 is a diagram showing this commonly used structure for a strategic framework.

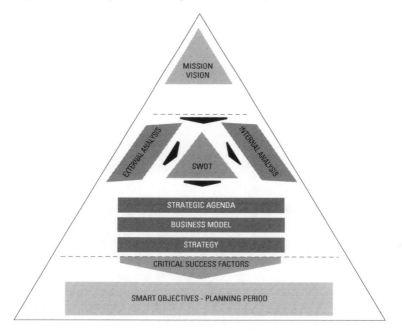

Figure 2.3   Strategy formulation diagram, from higher goals to objectives for the planning period

A BTF project assumes the availability of a strategy that provides adequate direction. If there is no strategy at all, then it is preferable to formulate one first before drawing up a business transformation plan. If the strategy is not adequately clear, specific and known, then it should be further elaborated as part of the business transformation planning project.

In practice, you often find bits and pieces of the strategy spread across multiple different plans and policy documents. Part of the strategy is often implicit and lies in 'peoples' heads'. Thus, the actual strategy is often diffused throughout the organization. Moreover, we frequently also see a number of independent functional strategies, such as the marketing strategy, the IT strategy, the HR strategy, etc.

It is precisely these existing strategic plans and policy documents in the organization that will serve as a starting point for expanding the strategy. The first task primarily consists of bringing together all of this information and analyzing it. The analysis mainly focuses on cohesion: are the strategy documents in line with one another, or are there conflicts? Structuring and occasionally integrating existing documents indicates where the strategy needs further clarification or expansion. In addition, this phase should also pay due attention to the strategy. This is because if you leave all of your options open, it is very difficult to make design choices.

Depending on what is already there and what is missing, the business transformation planning project will work out one or more parts of the strategy, such as those indicated in figure 2.3. Various strategic models are available to help you clarify and further elaborate the strategy, such as the Five Forces model by Porter (1980), the SWOT analysis (Sorger, 2011), the Value Discipline model (Treacy & Wiersema, 1997), the BCG matrix, or Balanced Score Card (Kaplan & Norton, 1993) and the Strategy maps (Kaplan & Norton, 2004). The different models will be more or less suitable depending on factors such as the preferences of the management, the issues to be addressed and the specific situation.

A discussion of all the strategic models is beyond the scope of this book. Many fine books have been written on strategic models (such as Pietersma et al. 2009; Mulders, 2014; Ten Have, 2003). The sections below cover the various parts of the strategy included in figure 2.3 using a combination of common strategic models.

2.1.1 Mission, core values and vision
Because the mission and core values will only be amended during a fundamental strategic reorientation, the business transformation planning process will rarely tinker significantly with these aspects. However, they will in fact be included in the definition of the strategy because the vision and strategy do indeed follow from the mission and core values.

The mission, vision and core values for an organization describe the 'essence' of an organization. The mission and core values are stable and only change in the event of a fundamental strategic reorientation. Although the vision of an organization is less durable, it will largely remain unchanged over the short to medium term. Thus, the mission, vision and core values comprise the foundation for the business strategy.

The mission of an organization describes its raison d'être and identity. A brief statement (also known as a *mission* or *mission statement*) defines the fundamental objectives of the organization and describes what the organization has to offer to its clients and stakeholders. The mission answers the question: why do we do what we do?

Familiar examples of a mission or mission statement are:

"To make people happy." (Walt Disney)
- No cynicism
- Nurturing and promulgation of "wholesome American values"
- Creativity, dreams and imagination
- Fanatical attention to consistency and detail
- Preservation and control of the Disney "magic"

"Improving people's lives through meaningful innovation" (Philips)

"Google's mission is to organize the world's information and make it universally accessible and useful." (Google)

"Campina adds value to milk." (Campina)

"To inspire and nurture the human spirit – one person, one cup and one neighborhood at a time." (Starbucks)

In addition to the mission, the core values of the organization are also stable. The core values describe the desired mentality, nature and behavior of the organization. They define what the organization stands for, who they want to be and what they believe in.

An organization's vision is derived from its mission. The difference between the mission and the vision is that a mission tells you what the organization wants to *stand* for, and the vision tells you where the organization wants to *go*. Whereas the mission mainly has to do with identity, the vision indicates the organization's ambition for the medium to long term: how does the organization plan to achieve the mission? Thus, a vision provides a picture of the desired situation for which the organization is striving.

A vision consists of three key components (Kaplan & Norton, 2008):
1. A challenging long-term objective: the objective should not be too easy to achieve and is based on a future vision;
2. A set market reach, the market segment or segments that are served;
3. A timeframe for achieving the objective.

Mission

We create the vital financial future that people deserve.

Vision

We provide trend-setting financial solutions for employers and employees. We set the bar in the Netherlands. In other countries, we are the innovator in the market.

Core values

Purity: The core value of Purity suits MN well. No-nonsense mentality, no pretences. We are simple and modest. We do not shout from the rooftops.

'Purity' means being open and forthright, and clear and unambiguous in communication with ourselves and our stakeholders – and it means sustainable and responsible behavior.

Passion: 'Passion' means involvement and the power of experience We want to come across as powerful and self-aware. We are proud of where we came from *and* of what we do every day.

We all bear responsibility for representing the MN brand to each other and our clients. We always go the extra mile for our clients. We work with passion!

Performance: 'Performance' means ambition and focus on innovation. Adaptability to change, with our sights set on results. We work hard at this and are proud of our work.

(Source for original Dutch version: www.mn.nl)

We have seen a great deal of discussion surrounding the usefulness and need for mission statements and visions (such as in Sinek, 2011), and varying degrees of significance are given to them in practice. We base our discussion on the definitions of Kaplan & Norton (2008). The mission, the core values and the vision are only of significance to the organization if they are based on ideas and ambitions shared within the organization. They should definitely not remain mere hollow phrases.

Whereas the vision sets out *what* the organization wants to achieve, the strategy indicates *how* the organization wants to achieve this ambition. The strategy indicates what the organization must do and what approach it will take. The steps below provide you with a basic guidance in the drafting and/or fine-tuning of the strategy.

2.1.2 Internal and external analysis

Strategic analyses primarily examine the internal and external characteristics and variables to be taken into consideration in the further expansion of the strategy. The purpose of internal and external analyses is to determine the orientation of the strategy and the objectives: what external developments should be taken into account or anticipated? What do the environment and stakeholders expect? What are competitors doing? What do customers value? What are we good at, and what are we not so good at? Strategic analyses can be conducted at different levels of aggregation. Some commonly used external analysis methods are:

- Analysis at the macro level: DESTEP analysis. DESTEP is an acronym for: Demographic, Economic, Social, Technological, Ecological and Political factors;
- Analysis at the meso level: The Five Forces model by Porter (Porter, 1980);
- Analysis at the micro level: benchmarking or the Strategy Canvas by Blue Ocean (Kim & Mauborgne, 2004).

For the internal analysis of the organization, we have methods such as:

- The Value Chain Analysis (Porter, 1985);
- The analysis of core competencies (Hamel & Prahalad, 1998).

Figure 2.4   Strategic analysis delivers specific strategic options

By connecting the dots between the results of the strategic analysis, you can map out the strategic options for the organization. For instance, a SWOT analysis can be used to find combinations between opportunities and threats on the one hand and strengths and weaknesses on the other hand. This 'confrontation matrix' provides offensive, defensive, investment and divestment options. Figure 2.5 shows an example of a confrontation matrix.

In practice, these internal and external analyses have already been made in the formulation of the strategy. For this reason, the BTF typically only uses them to validate or supplement the strategy.

2.1.3 The strategic agenda

The strategic agenda helps to clarify the direction of change by providing a general outline of the situation that the organization wants to achieve (Kaplan & Norton, 2008). By showing the differences from the current situation, the organization gets a picture of the steps that it wants to take to achieve its ambitions. This does not have to be very complex or all-encompassing: it can be described on a single sheet of A4 paper, for instance. (See also figure 2.6.) The strategic agenda is excellently suited for engaging with employees of the organization to discuss the necessary direction for change. It may create a sense of urgency and help determine the feasibility of the direction for change at a higher level.

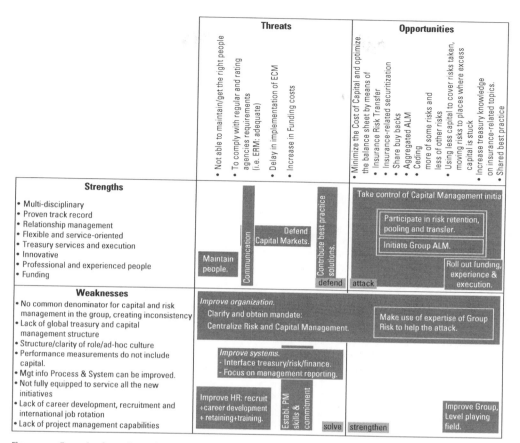

Figure 2.5   Example of a confrontation matrix for determining the strategic options

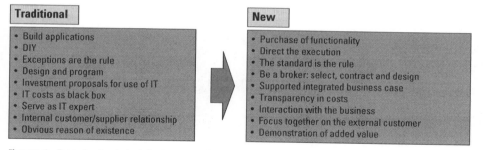

Figure 2.6   Example of a strategic business transformation agenda for an IT organization according to Kaplan & Norton

2.1.4   The business model

A business model shows how the organization creates value by allocating its most important resources, partnerships and competencies for a unique offer to its clients. The organization maintains a relationship with customers. The organization uses channels to provide products and services. The revenue model shows how the organization receives compensation for the allocation of resources and serving its clients. The difference between costs and revenue is the profit, which is partly reinvested in reinforcing resources, competencies and partnerships.

In this way, a business model actually describes an organization's formula for success, in general terms. One method for developing or testing the business model is the Business Model Canvas (Osterwalder & Pigneur, 2010).

Along with the strategic agenda, the business model is a powerful tool for concise formulation of the strategic ambitions, and for communicating about these with both management and employees. Together, the strategic agenda and the business model can be used to concisely formulate the strategy in a 'strategy statement' (Kaplan & Norton, 2008) or in 'strategic intent' (Hamel & Prahalad, 1998).

Business Model Canvas example: BMW's DriveNow

Introduction
The automotive industry is facing several challenges. Turnover is falling, customer needs are changing, and environmental standards are ever increasing. Thus, we are also seeing different business models in the automotive industry. Business models about more than just selling cars.

BMW's DriveNow
The business model for BMW's DriveNow is a service that launched in 2013 in San Francisco: fully electric driving by the minute based on car sharing. See figure 2.7. How does BMW create value with DriveNow and what do we find interesting and inspiring about this business model?

Proposition
With BMW's DriveNow, you do not actually own the car, you just buy the right to use it. After use, you can park the car at a charging station, without having to look for regular parking. A special app tells you where available cars, parking places and charging stations are located. It offers self-service combined with BMW's top quality. Customers pay a $39.00 registration fee and 32 cents per minute, or $90.00 per day to use the car.

Who is the customer?
DriveNow targets residents of San Francisco who want to use a car, but who do not want to own one, and who prefer environmentally friendly living.

How is valued created?
The core activities of DriveNow are: (1) manage and develop applications (2) use feedback from customers to improve the service and (3) enter into partnerships to create value. Key resources that BMW uses are 70 ActiveE cars, 8 DriveNow stations and investments from BMW i Ventures – a venture capital company set up by the BMW Group, focusing on location-based mobility services. BMW is working with several partners to create value for DriveNow customers. The main costs are marketing, loans for sustainable energy, app development and management.

The business model explained by the Business Model Canvas

The business model is elucidated by the Business Model Canvas. See also figure 2.7.

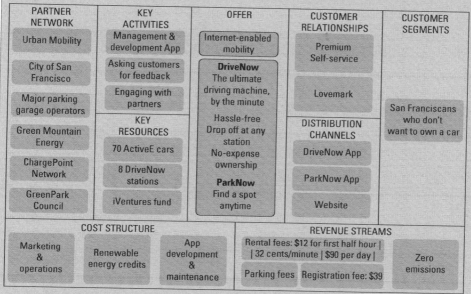

PARTNER NETWORK	KEY ACTIVITIES	OFFER	CUSTOMER RELATIONSHIPS	CUSTOMER SEGMENTS
Urban Mobility	Management & development App	Internet-enabled mobility	Premium Self-service	
City of San Francisco	Asking customers for feedback	**DriveNow** The ultimate driving machine, by the minute	Lovemark	
Major parking garage operators	Engaging with partners			San Franciscans who don't want to own a car
Green Mountain Energy	**KEY RESOURCES**	Hassle-free Drop off at any station	**DISTRIBUTION CHANNELS**	
	70 ActiveE cars	No-expense ownership	DriveNow App	
ChargePoint Network	8 DriveNow stations	**ParkNow**	ParkNow App	
GreenPark Council	iVentures fund	Find a spot anytime	Website	

COST STRUCTURE			REVENUE STREAMS	
Marketing & operations	Renewable energy credits	App development & maintenance	Rental fees: $12 for first half hour | | 32 cents/minute | $90 per day | Parking fees Registration fee: $39	Zero emissions

Figure 2.7   The business model for BMW's DriveNow (source: www.businessmodelsinc.com/new-business-models-in-the-car-industry/)

1. From car ownership to mobility: BMW notes that it is becoming increasingly difficult for residents of large cities to own cars. A business model based on selling cars is a major challenge. That is why BMW consciously decided on a business model geared towards mobility.

2. Business model validation: The DriveNow service in San Francisco is a major experiment to test out this business model in the 'real world'. After all, it is an all new business model. BMW is testing the proposition for carefree mobility (the right side of the business model shown above), as well as how well the ActiveEs work in a fleet (the left side of the business model, related to organization of value creation).

3. Partnerships: BMW opts to collaborate with multiple key partners to provide value to customers. Active cooperation can provide added-value. At the same time, these partnerships are also valuable for the partners themselves (it is a win/win situation).

4. Organized as a start-up: The business model is being implemented separately from the current BMW Group business model. DriveNow was set up by the i Ventures Capital Company. BMW i Ventures uses all of the resources of the BMW organization, but it also enjoys the versatility of a startup. This is a good example of how companies can organize innovation and entrepreneurship.

(Source: http://www.businessmodelsinc.nl)

2.1.5   Critical success factors and strategic objectives

In addition to being communicable, a well formulated and supported strategy must also be measurable and controllable. To this end, strategies are elaborated into goals, Critical Success Factors (CSFs) and Key Performance Indicators (KPIs). A goal is a predefined ambition that an organization wants to achieve. A CSF is a characteristic that is essential to achieving these goals (Rockart, 1979). These factors are so significant that they require additional attention from strategic governance. Each goal can be operationalized in one or more CSFs.

Some commonly used tools to operationalize the strategy into goals and CSFs are the strategy map (Kaplan & Norton, 2004) and the Balanced Score Card (Kaplan & Norton, 1993). The four perspectives from the Balanced Score Card (BSC) provide a sound structure for defining goals, CSFs and KPIs:
• Goals from a financial perspective, such as turnover and profit targets;
• Goals from the customer perspective, such as customer satisfaction or retention;
• Goals from an internal perspective, such as efficiency targets;
• Goals from the learning & growth perspective; some examples here would be objectives related to human resources or information systems.

The strategy map plots out the interrelationships between these four perspectives by showing the value creation process through applying cause-effect relationships between the goals. This creates a goal tree which tells you which goals or sub-goals must be achieved in order to achieve a higher-level goal. In a strategy map, these goal trees can also be grouped into strategic themes to clarify which goals must be achieved for a specific strategic theme. This gives rise to a communication tool. See Figure 2.8.

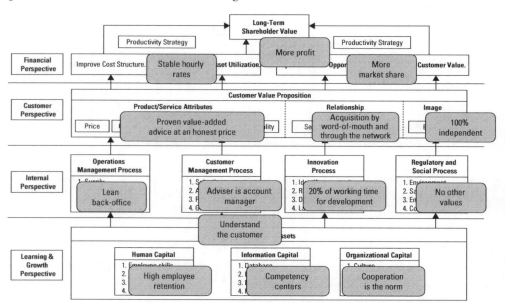

Figure 2.8   Example of a strategy mapped out for a consulting firm based on the Kaplan & Norton strategy map

In order to determine whether an organization actually meets its goals, each CSF is elaborated into one or more 'Key Performance Indicators' (KPIs). Based on these KPIs, dashboards can be constructed and used to report on the CSFs that are important to the organization. In this way, an organization can keep an eye on the progress of the strategy. See Figure 2.9.

		CSF result			KPI result	
Financial	RF1.	Reduction in costs per customer		RF1.	-20% with respect to 2014	
	RF2.	Gross profit increase		RF2.1	+25% with respect to 2014	
				RF2.2	20% of the gross margin from others' products	
Customer	RK1.	Focus strategy on business customers		RK1.1	All customers are divided up into appropriate segments	
				RK1.2	Target groups/segments served via the right channel.	
				RK1.3	Each segment contributes to the net profits	
	RK2.	Increase customer satisfaction and loyalty		RK2.1	Corporate, 85% retention	
				RK2.2	Consumers, 20% less churn compared to the market	
	RK3.	Growth in consumer market		RK3.1	Number-5 player in the Netherlands (by market share)	
				RK3.2	2016: 650,000 customers	
				RK3.3	50% growth compared to 2014	
Internal	RI1.	Operational Efficiency		RI1.1	One touch 95%	
				RI1.2	First time right 90% customer	
				RI1.3	9,000 customers per FTE	
				RI1.4	Reduction in IT …%	
	RI2.	Personalized propositions, B2B/B2C				
	RI3.	Improve Time-to-Market		RI3.1	New propositions within 4 weeks (80%)	
				RI3.2	Product changes implemented within 2 weeks (95%)	
Growth (innovation/ learning perspective)	RG1.	Right culture and competencies (entrepreneurship)				
	RG2.	Cooperation		RG2.1	Independent cross-disciplinary teams	
				RG2.2	Partnerships: 5 implemented	
	RG3.	Successful launching of innovations				
	RG4.	Proud employees		RG4.1	Employee satisfaction	

Figure 2.9   Example of a BSC dashboard

After going through the aforementioned steps and having the elaborated strategy defined or redefined by the management, the strategy will be specified and provide adequate direction for shaping the business transformation. Incidentally, this does not mean that you will not be regularly adjusting the strategy and its details in the further elaboration of the BTF. When engineering the desired business transformation, it sometimes turns out that the underlying strategy does not actually provide enough direction. In such cases, the strategy will have to be clarified further.

2.2   Formulation of guiding principles for testing current design choices and making new ones

Starting from the drawing up of the inventory and any fine-tuning of the strategy and objectives, it would be too large a step to make immediate pronouncements on the design of the services, processes and information systems and IT infrastructure. We need specific policy statements in order to assess whether the current design of services, processes and information systems and IT infrastructure meets the future vision, in addition to developing new design alternatives for these aspects.

If projects are derived from strategic goals too quickly, there is a risk that the definition and goal of the project will not be clear enough and the target situation will not yet be known. This may delay the start of the project because a great deal of discussion will be needed first in order to clarify the goal, definition and end result. In this case, there is also a chance that the project will have to be adjusted regularly during its lead time because the understanding of the goals and the end result to be achieved will change over the course of the project. Projects with names like 'The New Way of Working', 'Customer Orientation', 'Knowledge Management', 'Front Office', 'Business-Oriented Working', 'External Collaboration', etc., are often defined based on strategic goals or themes of the same names.

In other words, change activities cannot be derived directly from the strategy because it is too big a step, in light of the current complexity and dynamics in and around organizations. Formulating guiding principles and elaborating the desired target situation using the BTF reduces the risk of project delays or deviations in results due to lack of clarity over goals, definitions and the end result to be achieved.

Guiding principles are derived from the strategy and clarify the requirements and expectations people have, or should have, regarding the desired design for the organization. Guiding principles often take the form of policy statements. The BTF divides these into four categories:
1. Customers & Services;
2. Processes & Organization;
3. Information & Applications;
4. IT Infrastructure & Facilities.

Guiding principles are used to test the current design of the organization against the strategy and to provide direction for the target design of the organization. This means that the guiding principles restrict freedom of choice for the target design of the organization.

In general, guiding principles tend to be more or less binding upon the business units for which they are intended. You can use these for the intentional creation of degrees of freedom and, on the other side of the coin, for an indication of definitions and requirements. This is also indicated by the 'tight/loose' nature of policy. The policy formulation is 'looser' if more autonomy is permitted, and 'tighter' if, for example, synergy benefits need to be harnessed.

Well-formulated guiding principles are not mere slogans. A guiding principle is well-formulated if:
• It has a visible relationship with a strategy (strategic goal, theme or CSF);
• The guiding principle is clearly explained;

- The potential implications of the guiding principle are clear (in general terms);
- The guiding principle is specific to the organization or organizational unit in question;
- The relationship with other guiding principles is clear and consistent.

Table 2.1 gives some examples of guiding principles.

Table 2.1   Examples of guiding principles for the various aspects of running a business

Customers & Services	Processes & Organization	Information & Applications	IT infrastructure & Facilities
Local branches can enhance services according to their own understanding within boundaries defined nationally.	Decentralized branches have the option to use shared services.	Reporting systems meet the centrally imposed guidelines for data exchange.	Local infrastructure must meet the centralized requirements for IT architecture.
Our product line consists of a maximum of 10 products and a maximum of 3 variants per product.	All fulfillment processes are implemented in an automated manner to the greatest extent possible.	All customer data is included in the centralized CRM system.	Connections with third parties meet the information security policy.
Distribution costs are always transparent to the end customer.	Each team chooses a team leader from its own circle.	Bespoke systems are only permitted following approval from management.	The 'single sign-on' principle applies to access to all components of the information systems and IT infrastructure.
Data received through one media channel does not have to be retrieved again through another channel.	Every media channel has access to the same information.	In correspondence, digital and other data is made media-specific as far downstream as possible.	All infrastructure hosting in a country is in the same location and with the same provider.

'Bad' guiding principles are not specific and/or do not provide direction. Table 2.2 gives some examples of 'good' and 'bad' guiding principles.

Table 2.2   Examples of well-formulated and poorly formulated guiding principles

Not good	Good
In 2018 we will offer our products and services primarily through online channels. (This is an objective, not a guiding principle.)	Example: products are standardized and simplified for an online offer.
Applications meet legal rules and regulations.	Example: automated monitoring of the progress of work activities or statutory response times.
Processes are customer-oriented.	Example: information on the status and progress of customer requests and orders is available for customers in real-time.

Guiding principles follow on from the strategic goals and CSFs. For the formulation of guiding principles, we use the BTF: for a strategic objective, we examine – for each aspect of running a business – which guiding principles can clarify it in greater detail. For each guiding principle, we then determine whether interrelated guiding principles can be formulated in other columns. We must have consistency both with the strategy (vertical) and across all aspects (horizontal). For instance, if a guiding principle for processes is formulated, then we also examine whether this may result in a guiding principle for Customers & Services or for Information & Applications. In this way a set of interrelated guiding principles is formulated as a whole, which provides direction for the desired design of the organization in which the strategic issue can be resolved. Drafting guiding principles is a difficult process in practice, but once a good set of guiding principles has been formulated, it provides a great deal of direction for the change activities.

2.3   Outlining both the current and target situations

When the guiding principles have been formulated for the target situation, the next step is then to analyze the current situation and prepare an outline of the target situation. For this, we use 'architectures'. Elaborating both the current and the desired situation in an enterprise architecture creates a visualization of the business transformation that is needed, i.e. everything that needs to happen to get from the current situation to the target situation. This picture of the content of the desired changes is necessary in order to control not only time and money, but also the quality of the change.

With the BTF, we prepare a number of architectures for every aspect of running a business, i.e. for each column in the BTF. (See Figure 2.2.) This describes and visualizes the aspects of Customers & Services, Processes & Organization, Information & Applications and IT Infrastructure & Facilities in the organization. This process also ensures there is cohesion between the different aspects and clarifies the nature of this. The architectures prepared in this way have the character of a 'rough sketch' and are intended to provide direction. They are certainly not blueprints. This means, for instance, that little or no use will be made of formal architecture methods, modeling languages (such as ArchiMate) or architecture tools. The emphasis is firmly on the visualization of the target situation. This must be clear to all stakeholders; they do not require any training in formal architecture methods. The modes of thought and the principles of architecture are, in fact, applied here so the desired target situation is in line with the guiding principles, is internally consistent and meets the principles of being future-proofed.

From this point of view, architecture is not a discipline reserved solely for architects and IT architects. Actually, every discipline in an organization is already working with 'architectures'. For instance, Marketing deals with the question of what services to provide to which customers, HR & Organization works with the organizational structure and capabilities, the IT department examines which information systems and IT infrastructure can be best allocated to which work activities, and so on.

Preparing architectures for the target situation provides a solid picture of the situation that the organization wants to achieve. In addition to this, architectures of the current situation help show us where the organization stands at this point in time. In the analysis of the current situation, any constraints are also mapped out. Constraints are points of difficulty for the organization ('where things get stuck), and which impede the organization in the proper performance of its work. The constraints identified are shown on the architecture plans, creating a holistic overview of the main 'hotbeds'. The same also applies for the 'action items; that the organization needs to work on in order to achieve the target situation.

One interesting question is when an architecture is 'suitable' to use in the business transformation planning process. Architectures are in fact nothing more than a representation of reality, which means that there is not really a 'best' architecture. However, there are a number of guiding principles that must be taken into account when drafting the architectures during implementation of the business transformation planning process:
• Architectures for the target design clearly meet the strategy and the formulated guiding principles;
• Architectures make design decisions clearly visible;
• Together, architectures provide an integrated view of all aspects of running a business;
• Architectures are relatively stable;
• Architectures arise as a result of collaboration between management, specialists and subject-matter experts from various units in the organization.

Chapter 3 covers architectures in extensive detail. It discusses the analysis and design of the different aspects of running a business, with ample use of architectures. Once the architectures have been established and reviewed, the next step is to formulate the action items.

2.4   Formulation of action items necessary to achieve the desired change

Action items are specific activities that must be carried out in order to achieve the desired change. Action items will come from both the differences between the current and target situations (the gap analysis) and an analysis of the current situation (constraints and opportunities for improvement).

In addition to these, there are several other ways to arrive at action items. For instance, action items may also be in the form of research requests intended to further analyze any matters that are in need of clarification, such as researching and elaborating solution scenarios. This is because it is not always possible to finalize all design choices within the lead time of a BTF project. Decisions that need to be made are also translated into action items. Moreover, the lead time for planning is not always long enough for thorough analysis, which means uncertain or incomplete items are also included as action items, such as the requirement to take a complete and correct inventory of all applications in use.

Previously identified action items are also included. We do this by making an inventory of what the organization is already working on. This information can often be found in the existing project portfolios and department plans. This completeness is important because when setting priorities, we must conduct a thorough examination of previously identified action items and of newly formulated action items. This way, scarce resources can be reallocated optimally based on the latest strategy, priorities and insights.

It regularly occurs in practice that an action item is formulated too generally, leaving it resembling more of an objective than an activity. This often stems from inadequate clarity in defining the changes needed in order to achieve a particular target situation. If this is the case, then it is vital to ask critical questions until an action item has been formulated that does in fact clearly indicate the specific actions to be taken. The litmus test is to ask the stakeholders how they would approach carrying out the action item in question. The test question will be: "If you were assigned this task tomorrow, how would you go about performing it?"

Therefore, the action items should not be limited to a list of ambiguous terms. Incidentally, bottlenecks and opportunities for improvement are not yet action items: they still need to be translated into actions to be taken. An action item is not properly formulated unless the following are clear:
- What needs to happen and what exactly will the outcome of this effort be?
- How will the action item resolve one or more constraints or contribute to the achievement of the strategic goals or CSFs?
- What element of the organization is the object of the change? For instance: the residential insurance product group, the intermediary distribution channel, the order process, the financial accounting team, the CRM system, etc. Action items are often shown on architecture models as well. This creates a holistic overview of the main areas of transformation and enables better testing for completeness.
- What kind of action item is it? For instance: preliminary research, decision to be made, implementation, point for further research, etc.

Table 2.3 gives some examples of properly and improperly formulated action items. This also clearly shows that sometimes too much is included under a single action item, often implicitly. In this case, it would be a good idea to formulate more specific action items.

Action items can be formulated in this way for each aspect of running a business. Consistency and cohesion between the different aspects of running a business are crucial here as well. After formulating action items for each column in the BTF, the second step is to look for cohesion and completeness along the horizontal axis. This typically results in major additions and improvements to the action item lists. Table 2.4 gives some examples to illustrate cohesion between the action items in the different columns of the BTF. Simply carrying out just one or a few of the action items will not achieve the planned end-result.

Table 2.3   Examples of well formulated and poorly formulated action items

Not well formulated	Well formulated
Improve management information.	• Expand monthly report for management with sales management information.
New privacy legislation.	• Determine impact of the new privacy legislation on the organization. If necessary, submit project proposal(s).
Service response times are unreliable.	• Determine average response time for provision of investment advice to consumers. • Investigate the causes of the variation in response times for provision of investment advice to consumers. • Make proposals for improvements to bring the response time for provision of investment advice to consumers in line with the standard. If necessary, submit project proposal.
Select new collections system.	• Conduct package selection to select a new collections system to replace the current one. • Implement the new collections system and phase out the current system.

The result of formulating action items is typically an ample list of activities. In practice, it usually features dozens of action items. This comprises the 'raw materials' for drafting the business transformation portfolio.

2.5   Drafting the business transformation portfolio

The business transformation portfolio brings together all of the action items and subsequently groups, prioritizes and plans these, as described in section 2.4. We call this the roadmap. Along with the business transformation strategy, the roadmap comprises the business transformation portfolio for an organization.

The business transformation strategy or change strategy is a cohesive group of guiding principles for shaping the strategy (De Caluwé & Vermaak, 2003). The business transformation strategy does not feature any specific interventions or activities: this comes later in the elaboration of a business transformation approach. Although it is highly critical to a successful business transformation, it would be beyond the scope of this book to go into detail on the formulation of an effective business transformation strategy. For this, please refer to the available literature on this topic, such as De Caluwé & Vermaak (2003).

In larger organizations, a BTF project often results in multiple business transformation portfolios that need to be implemented. By identifying multiple portfolios, an organization is able to distribute its resources across the portfolios in the first instance, and follow this by the prioritization of programs and projects within a portfolio with respect to one another. An organization with multiple business units will prepare one portfolio for each business unit and possibly also a 'company group' portfolio for programs and projects that are not specific to the business units (such as generic infrastructure).

> An insurance provider offers Non-Life, Life and Healthcare Insurance Policies. A BTF
> project for this insurance provider will identify separate portfolios for Non-Life, Life and
> Healthcare because the strategic priorities and choices differ between each of these. For
> instance, the issues in the application landscape for Non-Life are completely different
> from those in Life and Healthcare. In addition to this, the project also identifies a 'product-
> independent' portfolio that includes programs and projects that deal with generic
> infrastructure, such as workstations, the data center, networks and telephony. Each
> portfolio has its own governance, which evaluates, adjusts and prioritizes programs and
> projects annually.

The roadmap serves as the foundation for monitoring and controlling the implementation of the planned business transformation. A roadmap contains programs and projects which, together, implement the desired transformation. The roadmap is drafted in such a way that it maximizes the contribution to the strategic goals ('value') and makes the full range of programs and projects controllable and feasible for the organization.

The starting point for drafting the roadmap is all of the action items arising from the analysis of the current situation and the design of the desired situation. Translating action items into planning takes five steps, these being:
1. Cluster action items into projects and programs or put them in 'the line organization'.
2. Specify and define projects and programs.
3. Prioritize projects and programs.
4. Draft the roadmap.
5. Determine the business transformation strategy.

These steps are also shown in Figure 2.10.

2.5.1 Step 1: Cluster action items into projects
A group of action items will exhibit close interrelationships. For instance, they may be related to the same topic, or have a dependency relationship. The action items are grouped in such a way that they can be logically carried out as a project. In this process, each project must be independent, complete and provide useful results for the organization.

Action items should, preferably, be grouped in order to maximize interrelationships within action item clusters and minimize those between different clusters. Action item clusters can be based on various criteria, such as:
• By topic. Such as the introduction of a new product that also has consequences for processes and information systems and IT infrastructure, or the implementation of a new application that also requires changes in the processes and employee training.
• By the object of change. Such as the same product, the same process, the same organizational unit, the same application, etc.
• By business domain. This normally specifically involves the final responsibility of a single manager.

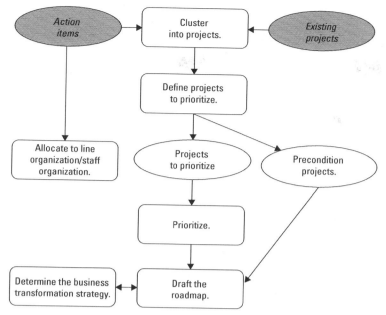

Figure 2.10   Five steps to get from action items to a roadmap

- <u>Based on the objectives</u>. This occurs if action items are interrelated with respect to the intended objectives.

However, grouping action items based on the objectives to be attained must be treated with a certain degree of caution. This can quickly lead to enormous 'containers' of action items. Clusters created in this way are overly complex, unmanageable and susceptible to a wide range of interpretations. In this clustering, the aforementioned objects of change – whether these are teams, products, processes or applications – are often part of multiple projects, which can place a heavy burden on an organization.

When clustering action items, it is also important to consider the cohesion between action items over different aspects of the BTF. After all, Customers & Services, Processes & Organization, Information & Applications and IT Infrastructure & Facilities are so intertwined that projects affecting only one of these aspects will hardly ever arise.

The aforementioned criteria are not necessarily mutually exclusive and are frequently used alongside one another. It is recommended not to execute the action item clustering process into projects too strictly because it is precisely the discussion of the interrelationships that exist between action items that results in the best insights. Discussion creates shared understanding and clarity regarding the contents of the action items and the activities that do and do not belong in an action item cluster.

Incidentally, BTF projects typically occur in the current context, where projects are almost always already in progress or scheduled for execution. In addition to the aforementioned criteria, action items can also be clustered with an ongoing project.

A number of action items can be allocated to the line organization
Some action items will also be part of the primary tasks of a department or business unit, which means no additional control from management is needed. Often, these action items come up during implementation of the Business Transformation Plan, but there is no reason to allocate them to a project. Examples of action items that can be allocated to line management are:
• Conducting market research;
• Deciding on a possible product development;
• Setting up data management.

If these kinds of actions have proved in the past to be difficult to take up in the line organization, and/or people in the line organization have had trouble controlling them, it may be decided to carry these action items out in a project. In this case, the responsibility remains with the line management in question.

The action items that have to be allocated to the line organization cannot simply be set aside. In order to guarantee that the action items will be carried out (in the correct manner), it is important to ensure proper transfer. The following must be clear: the importance of the action item, the goals it works towards, the manager responsible for it, the intended result of the action item and the timeframe for this result. These action items should be transferred to the responsible managers in a coordinated manner. The progress and implementation of action items allocated to the line organization that are actually preconditions for one or more projects or programs will be monitored from the business transformation portfolio.

2.5.2   Step 2: Define projects to prioritize
The groups of clustered action items are candidate projects. We use the term candidate project because so far, no priorities have been set or resources allocated. Each action item cluster takes a provisional project name, preferably a name that fairly specifically indicates the content and intended results of the project.

The projects are further elaborated into a draft project charter. The existing project management methods provide templates that can be used for this. For instance, PRINCE2 adopts the project mandate as the project charter at the beginning of a project. With the BTF, the general term 'project charter' is used. This takes up about one sheet of A4 paper per project and includes the key characteristics of the candidate project.

Key characteristics that should always appear on the project charter are:
- <u>Project name and description</u>: a brief description of the goals and activities in the project, derived in part from the action item descriptions.
- <u>Status</u>: does the project already exist and is it in progress (ongoing), or has it already been defined and planned but is not yet in execution (planned), or does it arise from the business transformation plan (new)?
- <u>Project phase</u>: some examples of different phases include the idea phase, the preliminary research phase or the implementation phase.
- <u>Responsible manager</u>: who is the executive? In the interests of 'durability', it is best to indicate the job title or position instead of a person's name.
- <u>Intended goals and results</u>: what contribution does the project make towards the strategic goals and CSFs and what 'deliverables' does the project provide?
- <u>Relationship with other projects</u>: is there a direct dependency or an indirect coordination relationship with other defined projects?
- <u>Expected lead time</u>: for both the research phase and the implementation phase.
- Budgeted costs and investments: what costs, other than internal capacity (see below), must be incurred? We often distinguish between costs and investments, given that this difference is important for a business case.
- <u>Required capacity</u>: how much capacity (usually in person-days) is needed from which employees or departments? A distinction is often drawn here between internal and external capacity, in connection with budgeting for out-of-pocket costs.
- <u>Risks</u>: what are the main risks in terms of, for instance, lead time, capital investment, political influences, scarce knowledge, number of interest groups, maturity of the organization, number of relationships with the environment, lack of a base of support, use of new technologies, available capacity, etc.?

All candidate projects must be developed into specific project charters to provide a picture of what the project involves for all stakeholders that is as clear and specific as possible. Only then can management prioritize the project in a reliable manner.

2.5.3   Step 3: Prioritize the projects

Before the candidate projects are prioritized, the 'precondition' projects are separated out first. Precondition projects are projects that:
- Are externally imposed (such as by laws and regulations, e.g. SEPA, Solvency II, etc.);
- Provide basic facilities.

This final project category generates a great deal of discussion as to whether such projects should be regarded as precondition projects. One reason in favor is that even though projects that provide basic facilities only provide indirect added-value, which means they often have low priority scores, they are in fact essential to the successful execution of other projects. One example of these kinds of projects would be the implementation of facilities, such as the creation of new accommodation.

Precondition projects do not necessarily have to be prioritized. The responsible management determines which of the other projects should be carried out first by assigning priorities to them. In addition to the candidate projects, this also involves prioritization of current projects. The relative importance of current projects must also be determined with respect to the other projects. After all, it may be a good thing if the analysis indicates that there are existing projects that contribute less to the strategic goals than originally thought.

We prioritize by scoring every project for added-value and risk. Added-value includes both the contribution towards achieving strategic goals and CSFs and the continuity of the organization. Criteria for assessing the added-value of a project can be derived directly from the elaboration of the strategy and goals. (See section 2.1.)

The risk assessment of the project is conducted in terms of organizational, economic and technical feasibility. Thus, this concerns the specific project risks and not business risks that are dependent on the execution of the project. This is because these were already included in the score for added-value. Examples of the criteria for prioritizing project risks include:
- Scope (in terms of costs or lead time);
- Technical and other complexity;
- Number of stakeholders;
- Knowledge and experience in the organization;
- Clarity regarding project scope and goals.

Project prioritization can be supported by visualizing added-value and risk assessments for the different projects in a risk/value matrix. (See Figure 2.11.) The assessment of added-value is plotted along the vertical axis and the assessment of the risks on the horizontal axis. We can then divide the matrix into four panes, featuring four types of projects:
1. High added-value and low risk → execute immediately.
2. Low added-value and high risk → set aside ('on the back burner').
3. High added-value and high risk → reduce risk, such as by dividing the project up, setting up a 'testing ground', hiring outside experts, etc.
4. Low added-value and low risk → only execute if resources, time and capacity are available.

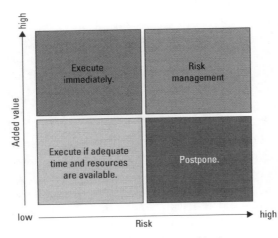

Figure 2.11   Risk/value matrix for project prioritization

Assigning priorities to projects proves to be difficult in practice because the level of abstraction, the sphere of influence and the development period may differ significantly from one project to the next. This is why it is vital to properly support the responsible management in such decisions. Project definition and value, and risk scoring are tools that we can use for this. However, discussions among managers on project prioritization are much more critical. This is how 'human aspects' are involved in the discussion as personal values and drivers. That's good - after all, it's about responsible management supporting the business transformation portfolio. Only then is successful implementation possible!

2.5.4 Step 4: Prepare the roadmap

The roadmap can be prepared using the prioritized projects. Just as with prioritization, drafting the roadmap is a responsibility of management/the board of directors. They are intensively involved in drafting the roadmap. The project team and/or the portfolio manager handles preparation and further facilitation of this process.

The start and end dates of all projects to be undertaken are worked out in a schedule. In addition to this, a plan is drafted for the required competencies and capacity, together with the necessary financial means (an investment and operating budget). The project charters provide key input into this. The planning in a multi-year roadmap is normally quarterly, but sometimes monthly as well. In practice, drawing up the planning often proves to be quite a puzzle and takes a certain degree of creativity. There is no single best formula for this.

Projects are initially scheduled based on the assigned priorities:
- Precondition projects are scheduled according to when they are needed. In cases of legal rules or regulations, for instance, we can calculate backwards from the required implementation date. The planning for projects that provide basic facilities depends on when the top priority project needs its results.
- The projects that scored high on added-value and low on risk in the prioritization are scheduled first.
- Next, the projects whose risks must be managed are scheduled.
- Finally, the projects with low risk and low added-value are scheduled.

In addition to priorities, it is also necessary to take into account interdependencies. Projects that have a low priority, but upon which other projects are dependent or may benefit from, will be scheduled earlier for those reasons. Before the actual scheduling, it is often convenient to create a matrix illustrating the dependencies between the projects. See Figure 2.12.

The roadmap must do justice to the assigned priorities and interdependencies between projects; but above all it must be feasible and realistic. The roadmap must take into account the organization's capacity for change. The capacity for change is an organization's ability to temporarily deploy people and resources to execute the projects in the roadmap. The capacity for change is typically expressed in monetary terms, but experience has shown that the availability of the right knowledge and experience determines an organization's capacity

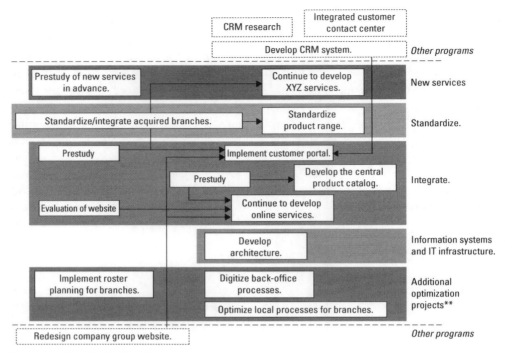

Figure 2.12   Example of a dependency matrix for a commercial enterprise

for change to a much higher degree. An assessment of an organization's capacity for change can be made based on key figures from previous years, such as the number of person-hours worked internally/externally, the out-of-pocket costs, percentage of projects implemented, etc. This assessment should preferably be made at the start of the business transformation planning process, so that it can be taken into account as soon as possible. See also chapter 4.

The project charters that have been prepared already include an assessment of the financial resources and capacity for each project. The planning process uses these assessments to determine how many projects can be in progress at the same time in a particular period without exceeding the organization's capacity for change. If it appears in the planning activity that the capacity for change is likely to be exceeded anyway, then choices will have to be made. Either the organization must increase its capacity for change (for example by external hiring or outsourcing), or the change requirements must be reduced (for example by postponing projects).

Clarifying how well the roadmap 'fits' with the capacity for change, often has a refining effect. Many managers are disappointed that various important projects cannot be implemented fast enough. However, it could be a grave error to ignore the capacity for change. Organizations that do not make choices but instead try to execute all important projects at once run enormous risks: schedules are not met, people and resources are not allocated effectively (due to fragmentation), results are not achieved in full, project scopes must be reduced, etc.

So far, everything sounds quite straightforward and clinical: clustering action items into projects, scoring projects based on added-value and risk, assigning priorities and scheduling projects based on priority and available capacity for change. However, a roadmap that comes about in this way does not have a 'soul'. There is no 'idea' behind it. Such an idea may involve phasing the ambitions of the organization into several steps. We also call this plateau planning, in which each plateau features a feasible situation that provides added-value for the organization (Figure 2.13). The business transformation strategy can also be a determining factor for this. An organization that opts for incremental change, for instance, will use a different roadmap and plateaus than an organization looking at a 'big bang' transformation.

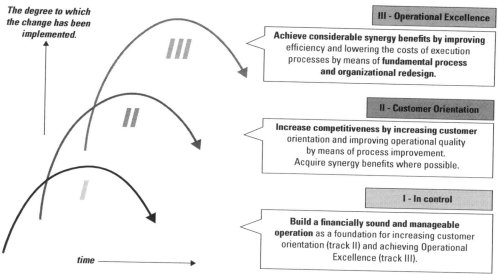

The degree to which the change has been implemented.

time

III - Operational Excellence

Achieve considerable synergy benefits by improving efficiency and lowering the costs of execution processes by means of **fundamental process and organizational redesign.**

II - Customer Orientation

Increase competitiveness by increasing customer orientation and improving operational quality by means of process improvement. Acquire synergy benefits where possible.

I - In control

Build a financially sound and manageable operation as a foundation for increasing customer orientation (track II) and achieving Operational Excellence (track III).

Figure 2.13 Example of a plateau approach in a multi-year plan

One common choice in determining the plateaus is explicitly taking into account the limited experience or suboptimal reputation of the organization with regard to change. This may, for instance, result in an increasing level of ambition in the roadmap. In this process, a lower rate of change is taken into consideration for the first year and complex projects with a relatively high risk are not initiated. The opposite also occurs, such as with a product rationalization, in which the most complicated project comes first. This is based on the presumption that: "if this works, everything else will fall into place."

2.6 Summary

Successful business transformations start with the design and planning of the change. The BTF may serve as a key tool in this. On the one hand, it helps in continuous alignment of the strategy with the business transformation portfolio and on the other hand, in the alignment of the different aspects of running an organization: Customers & Services, Processes & Organization, Information & Applications and IT Infrastructure & Facilities. We use the

BTF to arrive at insight, cohesion and a holistic overview, to make the complexity of the planned organizational change manageable.

This chapter has covered how to use the BTF to align the business transformation portfolio with the strategy. In other words, the strategy is translated into a business transformation portfolio, which involves going through the BTF vertically. This 'translation' cannot be performed in a single go: it requires a step-by-step approach.

The first step is to define and, if applicable, further elaborate the strategy and objectives. The BTF assumes a clear and specific strategy and objectives. If these are not adequately in place, then this area will require additional attention.

The second step is the formulation of guiding principles. Guiding principles give direction to, or even restrict, the design choices with respect to the different aspects of running a business. Guiding principles are used to test the existing design of the organization against the strategy and to make new or adjusted design choices. It is important not only for the guiding principles to be consistent with the strategy and design choices, but also for the guiding principles to be consistent with one another with respect to the different aspects of running a business.

The third step is to outline the desired design for the organization, in order to achieve the strategic goals. We use architectures for this. The architectures for the desired design of the organization are intended to give direction to the content of the changes. In this process, it is also possible to make architectures of the current situation, which may include identifying constraints. The holistic overview and insight acquired enable points of uncertainty in the design of the organization to be clarified— points where choices must be made, where issues play a role and/or where change must occur.

The fourth step derives the action items. These are all specific activities that are necessary in order to bring about the planned business transformation in reality. The roadmap clusters the action items into candidate projects and then prioritizes and schedules them. During scheduling, in addition to priorities, we also take into account feasibility and dependencies between the different projects. The business transformation portfolio is made up of, not only, a roadmap but also a business transformation strategy. This business transformation strategy outlines how an organization wants to go about achieving the change. Based on the business transformation strategy, as well as on past experience, ambitions for the organization, etc., plateaus can be identified and used to phase and schedule the projects.

The business transformation planning process is completed by drafting a business transformation portfolio. However, it will become clear that this is 'only' the beginning. After all, the business transformation portfolio must be implemented. The extent to which the business transformation portfolio is complete ultimately determines the extent to which an organization is able to achieve its strategy. At the end of the day, this is the only measure of success, but a good start is half the battle!

3 Distinguishing between the four aspects of running a business makes complexity manageable

Chapter 2 introduced the BTF. This framework is our tool to design, plan and control organizational changes. Chapter 2 also further explained how to bridge the gap between strategy & objectives and the business transformation portfolio. It showed how to apply *vertical* cohesion in the BTF. This chapter will cover the different aspects of running an organization and their interrelationships and will show you how to apply *horizontal* cohesion in the framework.

The design and operation of organizations is highly complex. We can make complex matters manageable by breaking them down and trying to work them out piece-by-piece. This often makes it much easier to understand the interrelationships between the parts. For this reason, the BTF distinguishes between four aspects of running an organization: Customers & Services, Processes & Organization, Information & Applications and IT Infrastructure & Facilities. The framework represents these aspects as columns. (See Figure 2.1.) This chapter analyzes and designs the aspects separately and in relation to one another. This is the only way to make the 'translation' from strategy & objectives to the business transformation portfolio. In this process, it is vital to achieve completeness and consistency in terms of guiding principles, design choices and action items.

First, section 3.1 will discuss the interrelationships between the different aspects. The next four sections will each cover one of the different aspects separately. It should be noted that the contents of the business transformation plan are always specific to the situation. As will become clear, an enormous amount of detail can be elaborated for each aspect. For each business transformation plan, conscious choices are made that can be elaborated for each aspect, but also what does not *have* to be elaborated. The issues and opportunities at play for an organization will serve as guidelines here. For each aspect, we will provide some basic guidance for making choices.

Section 3.2 will go into further detail on the Customers & Services aspect. This aspect is about which clients the organization identifies, what products and services it provides to them and how it does this. Section 3.3 deals with the Processes & Organization aspect, which involves the work that the organization must carry out for its clients and services and how that work is organized and controlled. Next, section 3.4 addresses the Information & Applications aspect. Here, we go into detail on the data and information systems that an organization needs to support its clients, processes and employees. Finally, section 3.5 covers the aspect of IT Infrastructure & Facilities, which is related to the IT infrastructure and facilities needed for applications, the employees and the way of organizing.

3.1   The four aspects of running an organization must be analyzed and designed in relation to one another

The best way to begin is with an example illustrating the four aspects of running an organization.

The management of an insurance provider notices that the product catalog expansion has resulted in 'compartmentalization' in the organization. Depending on the product, customers now have to contact multiple business units. Each business unit has its own processes set up, its own organizational design and makes use of its own applications. For instance, each business unit also has its own point of contact for customers. Customers are increasingly uncertain whom to talk to. In addition to this, customers are not served optimally due to a lack of an overall customer insight, including knowledge of their specific needs and any products already purchased. To solve these challenges, the management decided to launch a program to 'tilt' the organization towards a more customer-oriented organization.

In this case, it means the organization sets up a central customer contact point for all customers, regardless of their question or request. The transition to a single central point for customer contact also means that the existing (fragmented) customer contact processes must be redesigned and that different requirements must be set for the employees involved. After all, the relevant employees will be expected to handle a broader range of questions and requests. This also has a major impact on data and information systems. The employees working at this customer contact point require complete customer insight, so they can see all of the products and services the customer has already purchased, any agreements made, past correspondence, etc. This also has an impact on the infrastructure. Because customer service is accommodated at a single location, all infrastructure facilities must be available at that location. In addition to this, the telephone system, and its infrastructure must be redesigned to ensure that all employees at the central customer contact point can do their work.

This example clearly shows that the different aspects are highly interrelated. The analysis starts with customer service. What is needed to improve customer service? Next, this appears to have consequences on the process design and on staff. After this, the consequences on the data and information systems are analyzed, and finally those on infrastructure facilities. Figure 3.1 provides a detailed illustration of the interrelationships. For any development (such as a more customer-oriented organization), we can analyze its consequences on the different aspects. This process follows the different columns in Figure 3.1 from left to right.

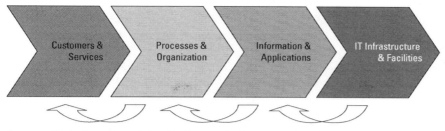

Figure 3.1   The horizontal interrelationships between the four aspects of running an organization based on the BTF

However, the cohesion between the different aspects of operational management works both ways. Untapped potential or improvements in one aspect can enable improvements or innovations in preceding aspects. We usually describe this with the term 'enabling'. This may involve unexploited potential already present in the organization. One example could be a complete CRM application that is currently only being used for relationship data management. But we must also examine the developments outside of the organization. Developments in the different supply markets for personnel, information, software, production technology, IT, etc. For instance, developments in the area of IT infrastructure enable all new models of software use, such as 'working in the cloud'. But this may also involve new organizational concepts, labor market developments, new production technology, innovative sourcing options, etc. These interrelationships are illustrated in Figure 3.1 from right to left.

The cohesion between the different aspects of operational management works both ways. Each aspect is connected to all of the other aspects. (See Figure 3.2.) It is clear that drafting a business transformation plan touches many different disciplines: from product design and marketing to infrastructure design. A well supported business transformation plan is drafted by representatives of the different disciplines. A cohesive design for all of the different aspects does not appear all by itself: it must be created. But how do we create a cohesive design?

We start by defining guiding principles for each aspect that are in line with the strategy. Next, we must examine the extent to which the guiding principles between the different aspects are in line with each other. In addition, a guiding principle in one aspect may also result in a guiding principle in another aspect.

Architectures are prepared for each aspect as well. We often begin by preparing architectures that represent the current situation. We can then determine the extent to which these architectures are in line with the defined guiding principles and whether architectures can be used to visualize the constraints. The guiding principles are used to prepare architectures for each aspect of the target situation. The architectures for the different aspects must be aligned.

Finally, the architectures must be used to define action items in order to get from the current situation to the target situation. An action item in one aspect often results in action items in other aspects.

The above may give you the impression that creating cohesion is a linear process, but it is not. In fact, it is an iterative process during which you must keep a constant eye on the interrelationships between the different aspects at the different levels (guiding principles, architectures and action items).

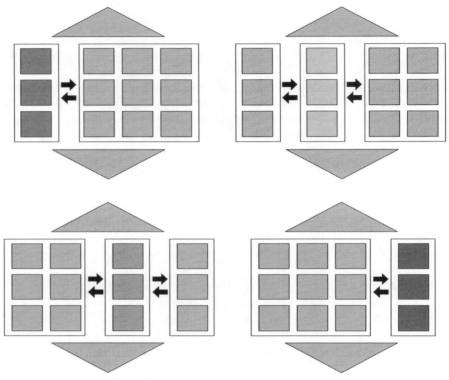

Figure 3.2   Interrelationships between aspects of running an organization in the BTF

 ## 3.2   Customers & Services: determine what the organization provides to selected customer segments

Without customers, clients, patients or citizens, your organization does not exist. All of your activities and your organization flow from this[1]. That is why column 1 in the BTF is Customers & Services, focusing on which clients the organization wants to serve, what products and services the organization offers to them, how it does that, under what conditions and to what quality levels.

---

1 When we refer to 'clients' below, we mean the purchasers of the products and services from the organization in the broadest sense. Thus, the meaning of 'clients' further in this book also includes 'customers', citizens' or 'patients'.

When elaborating the strategy, the first question to answer is how the organization serves its market. In this process, we examine whether the requirements and trends in the market are met and if the contents are consistent with the formulated guiding principles. It is critical here to look at the environment and the different kinds of markets and associated parties in the environment.

We consider the market the organization serves in order to make to prepare an inventory of products and services: which products and services does the market want from the organization and what are the organization's options for capitalizing on this. Incidentally, not all organizations enjoy the same freedom of choice. For instance, governments are obligated to provide certain products and services by law. However, they still have the necessary degrees of freedom with regard to additional services, quality levels and methods of distribution.

It is vital to keep our focus on the customer's perspective during organizational changes. The customer looks to the organization as a whole and has no idea how everything is organized internally. What's more, this is not even relevant to the customer. The changes that an organization makes must fit in with the bigger picture that the customer sees or must contribute to a better product or service, or the enhanced provision of a product or service.

Due to the importance of customers to the organization and the expectations they have for the organization's products and services, it is necessary to gain adequate insight into the design choices with regard to customers and services. Ideally, what would these design choices accomplish?

- *Make it clear on which customers or customer segments the organization will focus and with which services, in order to implement the strategy.*
  In the strategic planning for an organization, the mission and vision describe the justification for the organization's existence. Sometimes this is further elaborated in a marketing strategy, such as with a market analysis and a portfolio analysis for the product line. This is used as the basis for the choice of which customers to serve, the services to be offered and the manner in which this occurs.
- *Ensure alignment between customer expectations and the services on offer.*
  It is important that an organization understands what expectations its customers have with regard to the services offered. In this process, we should understand that not all customers are alike. So, we need to identify how customers differ from one another and what different expectations they have with regard to services on offer. Customers should be regularly asked what they think of the services on offer.
- *Provide insight into the different ways customers have contact with the organization and what demands are placed on the different methods used.*
  There are various media available to customers for contacting the organization, such as: face-to-face, phone, traditional mail, email, Internet and social media. There are also different times at which the customer comes into contact with the organization. What are the best media to use? This must be considered by weighing customer preferences

(not every medium is equally well suited to each moment of contact) against the costs associated with the medium (for instance, traditional post is relatively expensive).

- *Make it adequately clear what is expected from the services and what performance level is required, in order to design the performance and control of activities in the organization to reflect this.*
  The services that the organization wants to provide to its customers are realized by carrying out processes. The performance requirements related to the services are translated into performance requirements for the processes and organization.
- *Make it adequately clear what support is needed in terms of data and information systems in order to support customers in their customer-related processes and contacts with the organization.* Primarily based on the contacts with customers, you can determine what data and information systems are needed to support the organization and the customer in their communications with each other. Some examples here would be customer portals, where clients can perform all manner of transactions online (such as applying for insurance) and receive personal details, a knowledge base with answers to FAQs, management of dynamic content on the website, support for customer services in dialogue with customers, a customer profile, etc.

Now that we have a picture of what the design choices should ideally result in, we can ask which sub-aspects we should design for this.

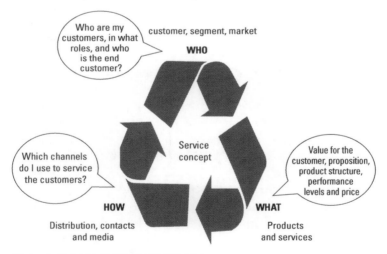

Figure 3.3   Sub-aspects of Customers & Services

The set of all design choices for the Customers & Services aspect is also known as the customer service concept. (See Figure 3.3). In order to gain insight into the organization's customer service concept, our experience teaches us that it is a good idea to design a set of four sub-aspects that relate to one another:

1. *WHO:* The markets and customer segments to which the organization wishes to offer its products and services. This is also known as the segmentation strategy. The segmentation strategy will be covered in further detail in subsection 3.2.1.

2. *WHAT:* The products and services that the organization will provide and the associated quality requirements and pricing. We explain this in subsection 3.2.2.
3. *HOW:* The distribution channels that the organization uses to offer the products and services, or the distribution strategy. Distribution channels are organizations or institutions that serve as intermediaries between the organization and its customers or end customers. We will return to this in subsection 3.2.3.
4. *HOW:* The organization's customer contacts and the media that it uses for such contacts. We call these the customer contact strategy and channel strategy, respectively. These two strategies are covered in subsection 3.2.4.

The above points already provide you with some guidance on making choices regarding where an organization's focus should lie when drafting a business transformation plan. For instance, if an organization has a problem with an excessive product catalog and wants to rationalize it, then obviously the business transformation plan should pay additional attention to the product architecture. In contrast, if an organization is serving its customers with a jumbled myriad of channels and is striving for optimal customer service, then it makes sense to have the business transformation plan that focuses on this.

3.2.1 An organization makes a conscious choice for the customer segments to which it wants to offer products and services

Which customer segments does the organization actually want to serve and what is distinctive about these segments? The answer to this question is vital in order to achieve high service quality. In order to gain insight into this, we need to focus on the terms 'customer' and 'customer group'.

Who is actually the customer? This seems like a simple enough question, but it can prove difficult to answer. Just take the example of an insurance provider. Is the intermediary the customer, or the policyholder, or both? And is the customer the one who takes out the policy (the policyholder), the person who is insured (the insured party) or the person who pays for the insurance (the payer)? In other sectors, the term 'customer' can be just as confusing, and different terms are used to refer to the customer. Some examples here might be client, patient or citizen.

If we are talking about the customers of an organization, we mean the end customers. This is important. The end customer, whether a person or an organization, is the one for which the organization is ultimately providing its products and services. The end customer is the end user (such as a repair company purchasing tools), the user (such as a baker purchasing flour) or the consumer (such as an employee working late who orders a pizza). The end customer determines whether the product or the service offers adequate added-value to justify paying a mark-up on the cost price.

The concept of an 'end customer' appears to be fairly straightforward, and in many cases it is. Let us take the example of a single adult who goes to get a haircut. This person decides to purchase the services, determines how the hair should look, receives the service him or herself and then pays for it. However, for many organizations, identifying the end customer is in fact not so easy. You may have found it strange that we describe the person in the example as a 'single adult'. Suppose instead that the person is a child going to get a haircut with a parent. The child receives the haircut, but the parent indicates how it should be cut and pays for it. Who is the end customer in this case? And what if the other parent, who is not present, also gave instructions for the child's haircut? In this case, we distinguish the roles of the User, the Specifier and the Buyer as separate roles from the end customer. These roles can be played by different people. Sometimes all roles are played by the same person, but frequently different customer roles can be assigned to different people. This is not always so easy to work out. Figure 3.4 gives a holistic overview of different roles that customers can play[2].

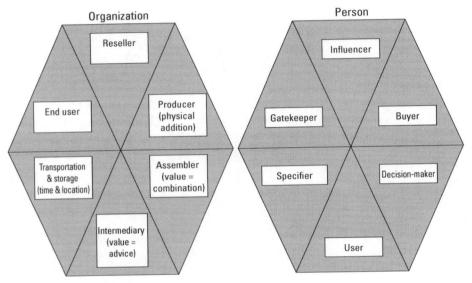

Figure 3.4   Different customer roles

Now that we have shed some light on the concept of the customer, let us turn to the concept of a market. A market is a group of customers that have certain characteristics in common which are relevant to the products and services or customer service. Determining the markets where an organization will operate is a strategic choice that is part of the business strategy, or the associated or independent marketing strategy. For more on this topic, see section 2.1 on strategy and objectives.

Categorizing potential or actual customers into mutually exclusive segments with the same characteristics is called customer segmentation. Customer segments are identifiable, stable, substantial in size, measurable and accessible. Segmentation is intended to provide optimal anticipation of the possible differences between groups of customers. Often, the identified

---

2   The model for 'person' is based on Blackwell, R., P. Miniard & J.Engel., 2001. *Consumer behavior, ninth edition*. The model for 'organization' was inspired by Giglierano, V., 2002. *Business to business marketing: analysis and practice in a dynamic environment*.

customer segments are represented using what are known as 'personas'. A persona is a stereotypical customer that represents a particular market segment. This enables optimal tailoring of the organization's product line and services to the customer's needs.

Customers can be divided up into segments based on customer value, customer share and/or customer needs. Customer value refers to the turnover or revenues that a customer generates during the period in which he or she is a customer of the organization. The value for the customer is a derivative of the customer needs: the sum of the benefits, both tangible and intangible, that a customer enjoys due to a purchase, minus the costs, time and trouble invested. Customer share refers to the share of all customer spending on a particular product group that is spent at the organization. Another term for this, especially in financial services, is the 'share of wallet'.

Segmentation by customer needs actually enables you to visualize the customer's values. At the same time, this is the most difficult segmentation to apply and requires a great deal of insight into customers' desires. Some examples of criteria[3] that can help shed light on different customer needs are:
• Geographic features;
• Demographic features (such as age, gender);
• Socio-economic features (such as education, income, social class, family situation);
• Purchasing and communication behavior;
• Psychographic features (such as norms and values, lifestyle);
• Purchasing motives and considerations.

For B2B markets, other criteria also apply, such as:
• Demographic criteria (sector, organization size, branch location);
• Operational criteria that are indicative of the support required for the purchaser (technology, competencies);
• Purchase approach (nature of the relationship);
• Situational factors (urgency of demand, application, order size, etc.);
• Personnel characteristics (such as company culture).

By expanding the concepts of customer and market above, we make it possible to draft targeted guiding principles and architectures for the different customer segments. Which customer segments are identified, what are the customer segments to which the organization does and does not orient itself, and what are the characteristics of the different customer segments?

If a bank wants to identify, for instance, the customer segment 'wealthy individuals', then it attributes certain characteristics to this customer segment. When is an individual a wealthy individual? And what should the customer service look like for this customer segment?

---

3 Segmentation criteria based on material from the University of Groningen by Professor P.S.H. Leeflang and Professor T.H.A. Bijmolt.

3.2.2 The products, services and service level of the organization must meet the customers' expectations

If you have a clear picture of the customer segments, then you can look at which products and services will meet the needs of these customer segments. To better understand this, we first need to discuss some other concepts in more detail.

Although there are 'one-product companies', most organizations are active in one or more markets and offer their customers different products and services – sometimes even under different brand names or labels.

Spreading risk is one major reason to offer different products and services. If one product does not sell well, then other products which are selling better can offset disappointing revenues. That is why it is vital for an organization to have a 'healthy' composition for its product range. The Boston Consulting Group matrix (BCG matrix[4]) is a well-known tool for analyzing an organization's product and service catalog. This matrix positions the propositions or products based on the relative growth of the market and the relative market share of the organization. (See Figure 3.5.) A well-balanced product range features 'cash cows', 'question marks' and 'stars'. 'Cash cows' generate income that can be reinvested in question marks and stars to retain market position, or expand in a rapidly growing market.

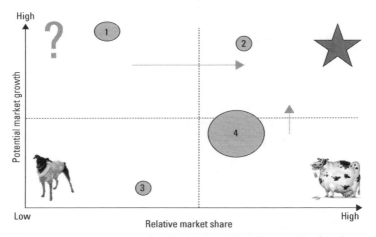

Figure 3.5   Example of a BCG matrix indicating the position of four products (1 to 4)

The products and services in the catalog can then be viewed at multiple levels, for example based on the three levels of Kotler & Armstrong (2012). (See Figure 3.6.)

Kotler & Armstrong (2012) distinguish between (1) the core value for the customer, (2) the actual customer product and (3) the total product. The core product indicates the essence of the added-value that the organization is providing, such as a train trip, an insurance policy, a selection of food products (supermarket) or customized software. Incidentally, a service

---

4   The BCG matrix was originally intended for strategic positioning of business units within a multi-division organization.

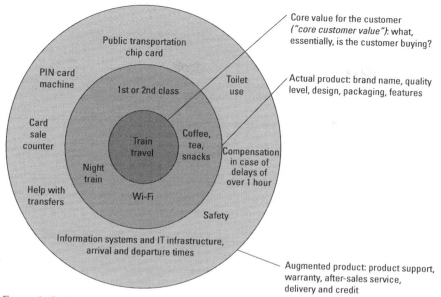

Figure 3.6   Products and services on the three levels of Kotler & Armstrong (2012)

must be of an intangible nature and cannot involve any transfer of ownership (e.g. a visit to the dentist for a semi-annual check). The core value for the customer is converted into one or more actual products. This level is about the features of the product or service, the quality level, the brand, the design and the packaging. This increases the added-value of the product or service for the customer. Some examples here would be a 1st or 2nd-class train trip or Wi-Fi in the train, as well as carefully built-up brand names. The third level is about how to ensure that the added-value for the customer is actually created and how to further expand the customer experience (augmented product). This may include product support, after-sales service, warranties, delivery and credit. Provision of information to travelers on arrival and departure times is part of this level, as is reimbursement in cases of delays exceeding one hour.

You can formulate volumes and quality requirements for products and services (this also applies to the augmented product level). Sometimes quality requirements are even stipulated by law. Table 3.1 shows the different kinds of performance requirements including examples. These performance requirements serve as critical input for the subsequent activities in the business transformation plan because the internal processes and applications (and ultimately the IT infrastructure and facilities as well) must be designed to deliver the volumes and meet the quality requirements.

Table 3.1   Performance requirements on products and services[5]

Performance	Example
Volume and variation	Minimum purchase, compose diverse combinations yourself (such as insurance policy coverage)
Quality and sustainability	99% of policies delivered flawlessly to the customer. Washing machine service life at least 5 years
Delivery time and delivery reliability	Production within 3 days, home delivery within 5 days
Price	Standard products for a fixed price; customization is more expensive. Price compared to competitors
Flexibility	Customization on request
Warranty and safety	Quality mark, online security, warranty, money back
Availability	Delivery directly from stock, day and night ordering, etc.
Relationship quality	Empathy, speaking to customers personally

For every customer segment, a separate proposition can be developed because each customer segment has its own 'unique buying reasons'. A proposition is the total offer for the customer (the augmented product) including its associated marketing. Propositions for different customer segments may differ in terms of additional services, quality levels for the delivery and/or the manner in which the proposition is made commercially available.

The following are examples of propositions with the same core product, but tailored to the unique buying reasons by means of the provision of information, the advertising or the packaging:

- Alcohol: as a fuel, as cleaning product, or for lamp oil (alcohol, possibly with coloring added)
- Spiced cookies: as a sandwich filling, with tea or as pie crust.

The proposition for a distribution partner is geared more significantly towards supporting the sales process to the end customer. Therefore, the needs of the distribution partner differ from the needs of the end customer. The basic ingredients (product components) may be the same, but the packaging (price, profit margins, quantity and delivery conditions) may differ.

Finally, we should mention the aspect of product and service 'breakdown'. This is a key concept which strives to achieve a balance between product standardization on the one hand and differentiation into customer needs on the other. Some commonly used names for this concept are: standard customization or perceived customization. Standardizing by sub-products and varying your product compositions for the customer can achieve a high degree of flexibility in your product offering without direct consequences on the production process. Standard product components are reused for multiple core products and propositions. This concept originates from the world of industry and is also now being applied in other sectors, such as financial services. One well known example to illustrate this concept is the IKEA cabinet systems. These can comprise of:

---

5   Largely based on N. Slack, S. Chambers, R. Johnston, 2010. *Operations management, sixth edition.*

- A basic cabinet (case) in different colors and dimensions;
- Installed components: shelf inserts in different colors, rods for suspended parts, shoe racks, built-in chests of drawers in different colors, etc.;
- Doors in different colors, dimensions and shapes;
- Handles in different designs.

Many of the product components of this cabinet system are also reused for other IKEA products. For instance, the handles can also be used for other cabinets. The attachment materials, such as screws and plugs, are standard and are also used for other IKEA products, such as beds, bookcases and kitchen units. In addition to this, the customer can pick the cabinet up from an IKEA store or have it shipped to his or her home, which means differentiation in additional services. Figure 3.7 shows yet another example of a product breakdown for an insurance provider.

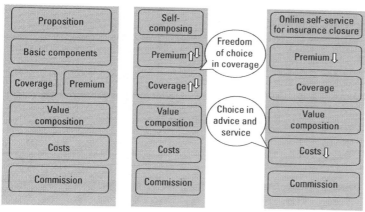

Figure 3.7   Example of product breakdown for an insurance provider

We can use the above concepts to draw connections between the different customer segments and an organization's product range and propositions. For the product rationalization of an asset manager, it would be useful, for instance, for the business transformation plan to clearly indicate which investment funds run by the asset manager are used for which customer segments and which investments funds could be traced back to which investment strategies.

3.2.3 Distribution channels are used to actually provide products and services to customers

If an organization sells its own products and services to its customers, this is called direct distribution. However, in many cases, an organization uses other organizations to sell its products and services. This is called indirect distribution. With indirect distribution, intermediaries are used to sell products and services. An intermediary may be an insurance consulting firm that sells insurance products from different insurance providers, or a retailer that has consumer goods from different suppliers on its shelves. Thus, multiple organizations often work together to get a product or service to the customer. This chain or organizations, which can range from raw materials extraction to final delivery to the customer, is known as the supply chain. Each link in the supply chain adds value, such as by processing raw materials into semi-finished goods, assembling semi-finished goods into finished products, delivering or installing finished products or providing services for maintenance.

A sound understanding of the position of an organization in the supply chain is crucial because we must provide not only for the needs of customers, but also for any suppliers and intermediaries. For instance, an insurer may provide second-line support to the intermediary when it sells more complex insurance products, or it may support employers with an HR policy to reduce absenteeism due to illness, which will remove pressure from the collective health insurance.

A proper understanding of the supply chain is also important in order to assess the added-value of each link. Links in the business chain that provide insufficient added-value run the risk of being eliminated. Organizations must be adequately aware of the movements in other links in the business chain: how are suppliers developing themselves? How are intermediaries developing themselves? And how are purchasers evolving? Are there any new entrants to the market who are 'changing the rules of the game'? Figure 3.8 shows an example of a business chain for an insurance provider.

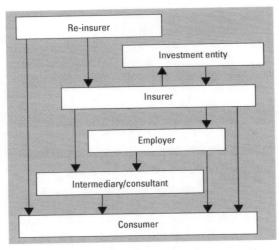

Figure 3.8   Example of a supply chain for an insurance provider

At the end of the day, it is critical to establish the connection between the organization's place in the supply chain and the consequences of this on the design of the organization. For each distribution channel, for instance, you can clarify how the organization should support this distribution channel and properly serve the end customer.

3.2.4   The services must be optimally aligned with the needs of the customers at specific times

So far we have mainly discussed customers, such as end customers, who purchase a particular product or service from the organization. The time of the sale is, however, just one of the times at which the customer comes into contact with the organization. For example, before a purchase is completed the prospective customer may have already learned a bit about the products and services of the organization and those of competitors and perhaps also spoken with an advisor or salesperson. Customer contacts also take place after the sale, perhaps in the case of questions, issues, malfunctions or defects.

Customer-oriented organizations strive for long-term and sustainable relationships with their customers. Winning over new customers takes a great deal of effort and it is often easier to retain existing customers than to create new business. In other words, preventing good customers from leaving may be more worthwhile that winning over new customers. Preventing good customers from leaving is called customer retention. The study by Reinartz, Thomas & Kumar (2005) shows that it takes a great deal of effort for organizations to bring in 15% more customers, but it takes relatively low retention costs to keep them in, while they account for around 40% of the profit! (See Figure 3.9.)

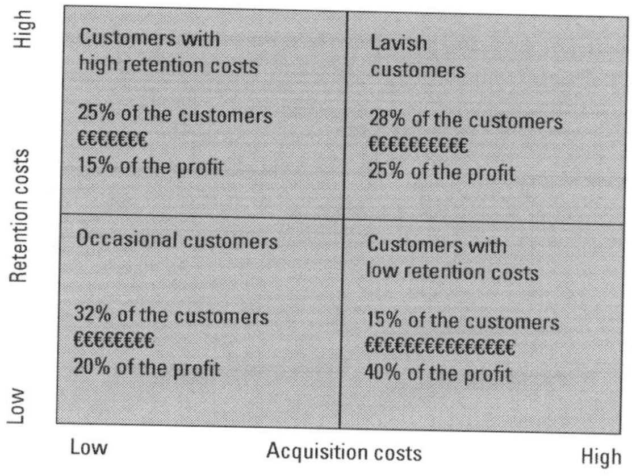

	Low — Acquisition costs — High	
High Retention costs	Customers with high retention costs 25% of the customers €€€€€€€ 15% of the profit	Lavish customers 28% of the customers €€€€€€€€€ 25% of the profit
Low Retention costs	Occasional customers 32% of the customers €€€€€€€€ 20% of the profit	Customers with low retention costs 15% of the customers €€€€€€€€€€€€€€€ 40% of the profit

Figure 3.9   Example of customer retention

To retain customers or increase their revenues for the organization by upselling, cross-selling, etc., it is vital for the organization to maintain contact with its customers. A customer that never has any contact with the organization after the purchase will have few reasons to remain loyal. That is why customer-oriented organizations pay a great deal of attention to the contacts they have with their customers, when they have them, why they have them and what customers expect at different moments of contact. We call this the customer contact strategy.

Key reasons for customers to contact the organization naturally involve a potential, future or past purchase. The route that a customer takes in this process goes through the steps of research, purchasing, use and evaluation. (See Figure 3.10.) This is often called the 'customer journey'.

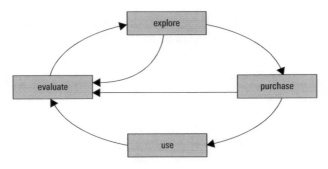

Figure 3.10   The customer journey

In each phase of the customer journey, the customer has different needs and experiences. Familiarity with the customer journey and the needs of the customer in each phase helps to align the organization's services to the journey. In this process, it may be important to determine all possible customer contacts for each activity and analyze the information needs for each customer contact. The information needs may pertain to, for instance, product characteristics (specifications for use, technical characteristics), pricing, contract conditions, distribution characteristics (media, accessibility, opening hours) and service characteristics (complaints, disruptions, warranties). In this way, we determine, for each product/service (or product/service combination), what information is important in the different steps of the customer journey. This insight may result in major changes to the design of the services and the associated processes and organization.

In many cases, it appears that customers orient themselves broadly in the research phase, often online and increasingly on social media. Many organizations capitalize on this by ensuring that they have a good 'online reputation', for instance by using specialized teams (also known as web care teams). These web care teams search the Internet and social media for customer opinions on the organization and respond to these, primarily to prevent damage to the organization's image, but also to capitalize on sales opportunities.

Of course, an organization can also take the initiative itself to contact its current or prospective customers. The times at which customers purchase products and services are often associated with events in the lives of customers or developments related to an organization (in the business-to-business context). Some examples are: moving house, having a child, getting your first job, retiring, etc. For organizations, this could include transfers of operations, relocations, mergers, IPOs, etc. Reasoning based on events provides a greater insight into a customer's needs: how can the organization use its services to capitalize on important events for the customer?

Contact with the organization can occur via several types of media: phone, traditional post, oral (face-to-face), online (Internet), email, social media, etc. However, not every medium is equally suited to each customer contact. In the research phase of the customer journey, many customers prefer the Internet as a medium, whereas for the actual purchase, they prefer a face-to-face meeting with a consultant or salesperson in some cases. During the customer journey, customers are increasingly switching from one medium to another. In this media switching, it is important that the customer experiences consistent services and information. Nothing is more annoying than first entering all kinds of information on the Internet and then having to repeat everything to a consultant on the phone all over again. Aligning the use of different media is also known as the 'integrated multichannel strategy' (Wilson et al., 2008). (See Figure 3.11.)

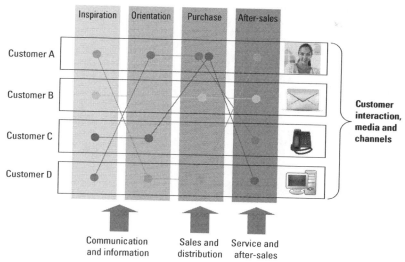

Figure 3.11   Example of an integrated multichannel strategy

Media differ in terms of their associated costs. The choice of the right medium involves weighing the costs, customer experience and accessibility of the organization. With banks for instance, customers are welcome to visit a branch office where they can have face-to-face contact with an employee. In many cases however, branch offices can no longer be reached by phone, email or traditional mail. Instead, customers must use a customer contact center. Whatever the choice, it is important that you always ensure that the customer is properly assisted and does not receive any conflicting advice or information. The factors of customer experience, accessibility and costs during each moment of contact should be carefully weighed-up: which media offer the required customer experience during this moment of contact? Which media offer the required accessibility? And which media can be used at acceptable costs? These choices are also part of the multichannel strategy.

The segmentation strategy, the customer contact strategy and the multichannel strategy provide an organization with insight into which customers it wants to serve, what the relevant moments of contact with customers are, what the needs of the customers are at each moment of contact and what media can be used for each moment of contact. Using this insight, we must then design the services, processes and organization around these moments of contact. The organization must ensure that it is accessible to its customers, not only at the times that the customer wants to make contact, but also by the customer's preferred method. For this, the organization has what are known as customer contact points, also called customer portals. In this context, 'customer portal' means a channel known to customers for getting in contact with the organization. Some examples here would be a website, store, consultant, a delivery service, a customer contact center, etc. An organization often has multiple customer portals. It is therefore vital that it is clear to customers when they should use each particular customer portal. To prevent customers experiencing inconvenience in finding the right customer portal themselves, it may be wise to bundle several customer portals together. This way, customers can always get to the same customer portal, regardless of the question or query, and are then effectively and efficiently connected through from that one customer portal to the appropriate contact point. The single customer portal handles first-line support, and the departments to which the customers are connected provide second-line support. For highly specialized issues, there may also be third-line support if the customer is passed through to a specialist.

It is important to have customer portals so your organization is accessible and recognizable for customers. The reasons why and method for using a customer portal must be clear to customers. The processes and organization of the customer portal must be in line with this. For instance, a customer portal that customers can access for all types of questions requires employees who are service-oriented, who can easily put themselves in the customers' shoes and who have empathic skills. A customer portal for customers with special questions requires proper specialized knowledge. Employees of this customer portal must be able to ask the right technical or other questions (or pass them on) and they should also have consulting and sales competencies.

To set up a portal that is recognizable to the customer, we must take the following points into account:
- The customer segment for which the portal is intended, such as for private or corporate clients;
- The services that the portal provides, such as advice or status information by phone;
- Accessibility of the portal, such as only during office hours, or 24/7;
- The media through which the portal can be reached, such as phone, email or face-to-face;
- The service levels for the service that the portal provides, such as a 'fast' portal for simple questions;
- The 'tone of voice' of the portal, such as empathetic and consoling for reporting a death.

3.2.5 Volumes and quality requirements are defined so the organization can be designed for these

Using insight into customer segmentation, customer contacts, distribution & media, customer portals and especially their interrelationships, you can see whether the organization is optimally designed for the customer service concept. For instance, an organization may have set up a separate customer portal for each product or service. In this way, customers run the risk of being constantly shuffled from one portal to the next, which is obviously an undesirable situation. Gaining insight into these inconsistencies, undesired overlaps and blind spots offers opportunities for potential improvements. We will take these potential opportunities for improvement up as action items in the business transformation portfolio.

To show the interrelationships between customer segments, products/services, customer contacts, distribution and media and customer portals, we can use matrices. Several matrices are available, such as the matrix showing the combination of products/services and customer segments (known as the 'product/market combination'), or a matrix combining the distribution channels, customer portals and products/services, and so on. Table 3.2 is an example of this kind of matrix.

Table 3.2   Example of product distribution matrix

Distribution / Product	Direct		Distribution partners		Account management
	Showroom	Online Ordering	Brand dealer	Independent Car company	Corporate market
Passenger car, A class	Personal contact, advice, knowledge	x	Continue to provide maximum support	x	x
Passenger car, B class	Set up location with showroom	Expand portal	Provide maximum support	Provide minimum support	x
Leased car	x	Develop portal	Develop proposition	Develop advice module	Reduce, direct to portal (self-service)
Bus, passenger transportation	x	x	Intro to service & maintenance concept	x	Focus
Transportation by bus	x	x	Intro to service & maintenance concept	x	Maintenance
Custom-built car	Personal contact, advice, knowledge	x	x	x	Market potential, set up a notification function from customization to standard

Incidentally, in general we often use matrices to visualize the interrelationships between the different aspects and sub-aspects. In addition to models, matrices are also an excellent tool for describing architectures.

3.3   Processes & Organization: how is the 'work' performed, organized and controlled

Section 3.2 addresses the question of which products and services are provided to which customers and in what way. To achieve this, an organization must undertake 'work': or in other words, processes must be carried out. The performance of the processes is organized and controlled in a specific way. This is the subject matter of the Processes & Organization aspect. Processes and their control are designed to provide added-value for the customer. The method of organization must support this. Making clear and effective design choices with regard to the execution and control of work activities, in an organization, are therefore crucial. If these choices are not clear, or not effective, this will impact upon the services. Employees should also clearly understand how they contribute to creating added-value for customers.

Below, we list six requirements that design choices should ideally address for the Processes & Organization aspect:

1. *Ensure that the design of Processes & Organization meets the requirements set for the Customers & Services aspect.*

   The requirements that customers place on the services may be concerned with, for instance, processing lead times or reliability. A process in which customers can take out an insurance policy online and in real-time without human intervention differs from a process in which customers receive personalized advice from a consultant. Processes can also be distinguished according to the customer segment, such as a distinction into serving corporate versus private persons. Processes can also be designed around customer contact moments. A customer familiarizing him or herself with a particular product has completely different needs in terms of advice, contact and information compared to a customer who has already made a choice and wants to purchase the product.

2. *Make it clear how to increase or guarantee the effectiveness of the processes, their control and the organization.*

   The execution and control of processes should ensure a high degree of effectiveness in terms of quality, reliability, transparency, predictability and flexibility.

3. *Make it clear how to increase or maintain the efficiency of the processes, their control and the organization.*

   The execution and control of the processes should, preferably, ensure constant low costs because they eliminate transfer times and excessive activities (for example by applying 'Lean thinking' (Womack, 2003)). A lower cost price is good for the organization's competitive position and makes it possible to invest and innovate.

4. *Serve as the basis for establishing the required knowledge along with the employee and management competencies and behaviors that are needed to execute and control the activities.*

   The processes in an organization are performed and controlled by employees and management. The execution of a process places requirements on the employees. A certain level of knowledge is required, together with specific competencies or skills, and a suitable attitude and corresponding behavior. Not all employees have the competencies to sell products, and not every employee is well suited to customer service. The same applies in terms of controlling processes. What culture is desirable? What management style should you choose?

5. *Serve as the basis for defining functional requirements on the data and information systems to support the work activities.*

   Based on the processes and control of an organization, we can determine the required data and information systems. The first thing you need to support execution of the processes is applications for automated data processing and recording. These applications must meet the specific performance requirements of the process in question. In addition to this, employees also have a particular need for information in order to undertake their work, such as knowledge databases, a customer profile or certain reports. Of course, the same also applies to management, who need certain management information in order to make decisions.

6. *Serve as the basis for defining requirements for the infrastructure to support the employees.*
Many organizations embrace 'The New Way of Working', in which employees can work flexible hours from any location. To enable this, you must make choices with regard to infrastructure, such as setting up a home or virtual workstation or enabling employees to work with different devices (such as tablets and smartphones). Of course, the locations where employees can work must be fitted with the necessary infrastructure. In addition, if employees can work from different locations, the infrastructure must enable remote collaboration.

The six requirements detailed above are all concerned with the interrelationships between the different aspects of running a business.

In order to get a clear picture of the necessary infrastructure choices for Processes & Organization, our experiences teach us that it is a good idea to design some sub-aspects that relate to one another. In subsection 3.3.1, we cover performance of the work in the form of processes. Organizing work is about work distribution and coordination, so we will go into further detail on this in subsection 3.3.2. The governance of an organization is the topic of subsection 3.3.3.

The above points already give you some guidance on how to apply focus in drafting the business transformation plan. If there are any uncertainties in an organization with regard to work distribution and coordination, then additional attention is required in relation to the organization of that work. In the event of specific issues in the area of governance, you can focus on these in a number of ways, for example by drawing up a governance model of the current and target situations.

3.3.1   An organization performs its 'work' by means of processes

When a customer purchases a product or a service, this triggers an internal process that results in the delivery and invoicing of the product or service. The organization performs the 'work' based on processes (provision of products and services). This is about creating added-value for the customer. Naturally, an organization must have a clear picture of the 'work' that creates the added-value. That is why a business transformation plan usually starts with drafting a well-organized process and/or business capability model. After this, you can focus on any constraints in the processes or capabilities, on changes to these and on the design choices that affect them.

We can define a process as follows:

> A process is an ordered series of direct or indirect value-adding tasks by a human or machine intended to produce a known result.

This definition indicates two aspects:
1. The result that must be delivered.
2. The tasks that must be performed in order to achieve this specific result.

These are also two ways to look at the 'work' that an organization must perform in order to provide added-value for its customers. The first way focuses mainly on WHAT an organization needs to do. For this purpose, an organization is depicted as a collection of capabilities. We define a capability as a result-oriented abstraction of a process or activity.

The second way deals with HOW an organization does 'work', namely as a chain of tasks. Both ways of looking at an organization are useful, and can complement each other.

Given that capabilities focus on the WHAT, they are relatively stable and independent of the design. As long as the organization keeps delivering the same products and services, the same capabilities will continue to be needed to provide added-value for the customer. Only if the product and service offer fundamentally changes (such as in a strategic change of course) will this be expressed in the capabilities.

Figure 3.12 shows an example of a business capability model.

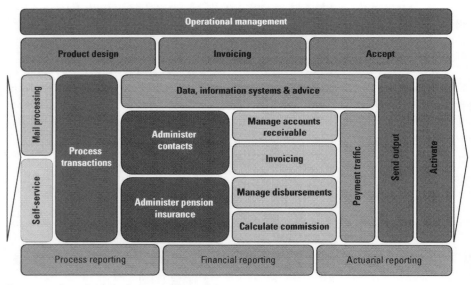

Figure 3.12   Example of a business capability model

Why is it useful to prepare a business capability model? A business capability model is helpful in the following tasks, for instance:
• Identifying synergy benefits by clustering similar 'work' and performing it concurrently to the greatest extent possible (using parameters where applicable);
• Examining alternative methods of process design;

- Assessing the organization model;
- Defining the general principles for information processes (see section 3.4).

One key design choice to be made, based on the business capability model, is which capabilities an organization wishes to carry out itself and which it seeks to outsource (in other words, what are its core activities and what are its non-core activities).

In addition to a business capability model, we can also draw up a process model. When drafting a business transformation plan, we examine the level of processes that is relevant to each situation and where the emphasis should lie. Processes can be viewed at five different levels.
1. Chain processes: an ordered series of services that different organizations provide to one another with the aim of providing a service or combination of services to a customer via a single organization.
2. Internal processes: an ordered series of processes carried out within a single organization with the aim of providing a service or combination of services to a customer.
3. Processes: an ordered series of activities that are performed within the same capability with the aim of making a specific contribution to a service that will ultimately be provided to a customer.
4. Activity: an ordered series of tasks that are performed, uninterrupted, by a single person or machine.
5. Task: the smallest identifiable unit of work, performed by a person or machine at a single place and time.

Often, the level of a holistic overview is adequate for a business transformation plan and, in terms of the level of detail, an examination down to the process level will suffice. The supply chain level will mainly be of interest in cases of supply chain issues or changes in the supply chain. The benefit of a process model is that it is easily recognizable for the organization. A business capability model is design-free and, thus, also more abstract. Figure 3.13 shows an example of a process model.

Figure 3.13 shows that we can distinguish between three types of processes:
1. Primary processes: these add value to the provision of products and services to the customer and therefore describe the service and production processes.
2. Governing processes: activities related to planning, control, evaluation and adjustment of the primary processes.
3. Support processes: activities that result in the availability of people, systems and resources to carry out the primary processes.

Each type has certain conditions and features that must be considered in the design.

The process model serves as a good foundation for determining where changes are needed at the process level in order to achieve the strategy. Based on the strategic goals for the

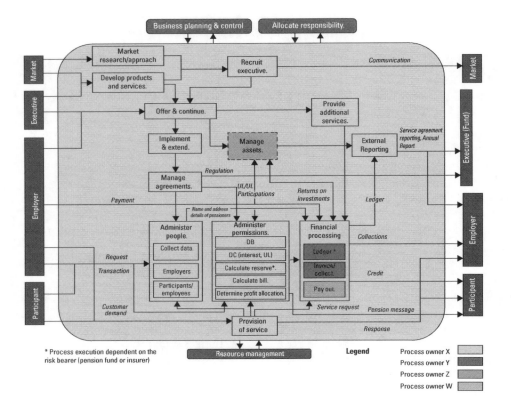

Figure 3.13   Example of an internal process model

organization and the formulated guiding principles, the processes will have different specific characteristics:

• *Customer/customer category:* are we focused on a specific customer category or customer? If the outcome needs to meet certain customer standards, it may be wise to group processes around a particular customer or customer category.

• *Frequency:* how often does this situation or case occur?

• *Mass versus series versus unit production:* processes may differ in their production methods. Processes may be carried out in large volumes, in a standardized manner and without distinction into individual orders (mass) or by individual order (unit). Series production lies in between these.

• *Routine versus knowledge-intensive:* processes may differ in the degree to which they require specific knowledge. Routine processes can be carried out automatically, while other processes require knowledge from highly trained staff. Is the process knowledge-intensive, or do certain quality requirements have to be met? If so, then it is advisable to shape the processes around the knowledge they require, as much as possible.

• *Environmental factors:* which environmental factors are important? Here we need to consider the 'law of requisite variety', which states that in order to adapt successfully to your environment, processes must have the same range of variation as the environment in which they are carried out.

Finally, we should note that design principles are important in determining the desired process design and improving the processes. For instance:

- *Lean Thinking/value added*[6]: each process must add specific value for the customer. If a process does not add value, then it is excessive (waste).
- *Straight-Through Processing (STP)*[7]: an STP process is carried out in a single go, uninterrupted and without human intervention.
- *Pull/Just-In-Time (JIT)*[6]: with Pull/JIT, the value is pulled through the process, rather than pushed. This means that the process is only carried out if an actual need arises for the result of the process. The opposite of Pull/JIT is production-to-stock.
- *Push/Pull Point (PPP)*: the Push/Pull Point is the point that indicates how far into an organization's process a customer order penetrates.
- *Medium Push/Pull Point (MPPP)*: the Medium Push/Pull Point indicates the point in the process up to which the selected process design is dependent on the medium used for customer contact. After the MPPP, the process has a medium-independent design.

Armed with these specific features, we can determine what needs to change in the process design in order to achieve the strategy.

3.3.2 The organization of processes divides and coordinates the 'work'

The organization of processes is all about distribution of work activities, managing dependencies between activities and delegating authority. Additional attention to this during the drafting of a business transformation plan is useful if there are constraints in these areas, or if strategic choices require the distribution and coordination of more work, or if the organizational design changes.

Distribution of work is handled by selecting an organizational structure. Management of the dependencies between work activities is handled by designing coordination mechanisms. Finally, delegation of authority means that responsibilities are allocated. We will cover these topics in further detail below.

1. *Design an organizational structure to divide the work.*
If an organization is growing in size, a time will come when the work can no longer be performed by just one person. The work must be distributed across multiple employees. This is the problem of division of labor. When work activities are divided up, you get vertical and horizontal differentiation.

The vertical differentiation is about the separation of management and execution. The activities are divided up into levels based on the 'price of labor'. The more qualified the work, the higher the 'price of labor'. This gives rise to a hierarchy of activities. When dividing work

---

6 For further information, please see: Womack, J.P. & D.T. Jones, 2003. *Lean Thinking, Banish waste and create wealth in your corporation.*

7 For further information, see: *Weske, M., 2012. Business Process Management: Concepts, Languages, Architectures (Second Edition). Springer.*

up into hierarchical levels, it is important to keep an eye on the number of employees per supervisor, also known as the 'span of control'.

The horizontal differentiation involves dividing work up according to similarity and/or similarity of results. Various criteria can be applied for this:
• Functional division: division of work by type or phase of execution;
• Product-oriented division: division of work by product or service;
• Geographic division: division of work into regions or countries;
• Market-oriented division: division of work by market or customer segment.

This division of activities is for those at the same hierarchical level. This means that for each hierarchical level, a different criterion can be selected for the horizontal differentiation. This may give rise to combinations of functional, product-oriented, geographic and market-oriented divisions of work.

Based on the vertical and horizontal differentiation, individual employees are divided up into the following bodies: line departments, staff departments, business units and teams. This is how the organizational structure takes shape.

The capabilities and internal processes provide a description of the work activities and an initial horizontal division of work. The capabilities or the internal processes can be projected onto the organizational structure so a picture arises of the distribution of work into departments and business units.

Based on vertical and horizontal differentiation, the organizational structure can be further elaborated into employee roles and functions. These define the expected results, tasks, responsibilities and authorizations. This level of detail is however only necessary in certain cases, such as a reorganization.

2. *Design of coordination mechanisms for managing dependencies.*
When hierarchical control is not adequate to manage these dependencies, additional coordination mechanisms are necessary. These dependencies can be coordinated by standardization or lateral connections. (See Hatch, 1997, for instance.):
• Coordination by standardization:
  – Standardization of processes based on, for instance, manuals and procedures;
  – Standardization of output by reaching agreements on the results to be achieved;
  – Standardization of knowledge and skills by means of training and education;
  – Standardization of standards by means of shared culture.
• Coordination by means of lateral connections:
  – Alignment by means of contact between employees, possibly supported by data and information systems (such as intranet, collaboration portals, newsletters, etc.);
  – Liaison role, by appointing a liaison employee who organizes and improves contacts between employees;

- Task forces or project groups established as temporary partnerships that are dissolved as soon as the intended result is achieved;
- Teams as permanent consultation structures;
- Coordinators/integrators, by appointing employees with the authority to promote coordination between employees and departments these employees can have coordination or management responsibilities;
- Matrix structures, by appointing managers with operational or functional authority in addition to line managers with hierarchical authority.

The coordination mechanism must match the complexity and scope of the coordination needs.

Coordination requires money and effort and therefore should not be used either too little or too much. If direct supervision is not adequate for managing the interrelationships, then additional coordination and standardization are required. If that is not adequate either, then additional coordination through lateral connections will be required.

3. *Division of authority for allocation of responsibilities.*
The division of authorities in the organization is largely determined by the organizational structure and coordination mechanism. It is important to distinguish three types of authority here:
1. Hierarchical authority.
2. Operational authority.
3. Functional authority.

Hierarchical authority is a direct derivative of vertical differentiation and defines the responsibility for the general state of affairs within a department.

Operational authority is the authority to give employees work assignments and address them regarding the results to be achieved, regardless of whether the employee works in the department or is loaned out or posted elsewhere.

Functional authority is the responsibility to maintain, develop and apply specialized knowledge and skills, for example through the provision of policies, guidelines and instructions.

In an organizational structure, where the principle of 'unity of command' applies, all three types of authority are united in one and the same person. In organizational structures with formal coordination mechanisms, such as the project or matrix structure, the three types of authority are distributed over multiple persons. In a project structure, the project manager has the operational authority, whereas the hierarchical authority and (normally) the functional authority lie with the departmental manager. In a matrix structure, the functional manager has functional authority and the departmental manager has the hierarchical and operational authorities. Clear allocation of the three types of authority ensures that everyone is clear on who is responsible for what, even in situations without 'unity of command.'

3.3.3 Control is handled by allocating decision-making authorities in the organization

The effective and efficient design and organization of processes is essential to the success of an organization, but these alone are not enough. Control is needed to ensure that the processes are actually carried out in an effective and efficient manner and that the customer is served. On the one hand we have extrinsic control, where the objectives to be achieved are determined, evaluated and adjusted. On the other hand, we have intrinsic control, where the employees are motivated and incentivized to achieve certain results.

Extrinsic control

Extrinsic control is based on the Deming cycle, a management control cycle of planning, doing, checking and acting (Plan-Do-Check-Act). This cycle defines specific goals and determines whether the goals will be achieved by performing the work activities. If not, then the work activities or goals are adjusted. Many organizations have management control processes designed for drafting strategic plans, departmental plans, annual plans, budgets, etc., and using these for overall control, as well as for collecting management information in order to oversee the performance of work activities and determine whether any adjustments are needed.

For management, the management control process is crucial for effective control. However, in practice, the reality is that management are frequently not in a position to evaluate the correct factors because they do not have access to enough information (of adequate quality). In such cases, it may be necessary to take a closer look at the management control process and, if necessary, redesign it.

Intrinsic control

Intrinsic control is about employee motivation. Employee motivation may be influenced by factors such as the pay structure, involvement, task enrichment, meaningfulness or other cultural factors. If it is suspected that there is an issue related to intrinsic motivation or the organizational culture, then we can use various models for cultural diagnosis and analysis to shed some light on it.

3.4 Information & Applications: the data and information systems that the organization needs

In section 3.3 on the Processes & Organization aspect, we addressed the question of what 'work' needs to be carried out in order to serve the customer and how that 'work' should be organized. The Information & Applications aspect is about providing optimal support for the services, the 'work' that must be performed and the desired approach to organization in terms of the data and information systems needed.

Having your data and information systems in order is a prerequisite for an effective and efficient organization. If the data and information systems experience problems, work in the organization can stall and services may be jeopardized. For instance, if a business-critical application is temporarily down, it will become increasingly difficult for staff to perform their work and, in turn, to contribute to the services. Moreover, the running of an organization is becoming increasingly intertwined with information processing. We can see this, for instance, in processes that are performed automatically without human intervention (also known as 'straight-through processing'), or in the embedding of data and information systems in an organization's products (such as with RFID tags).

Therefore, organizations usually invest heavily in information systems. This relates not only to investments in the purchasing or development of new information systems, but also in investments in the maintenance of existing information systems. So, how do we ensure that this money is spent on the right things? This requires a good overview of the design of data and information systems as well as the choices that need to be made to ensure optimal support for services, processes and employees. The following subsection goes into further detail on these design choices.

3.4.1 Design choices ensure optimization and alignment with the other organizational aspects

An organization uses design choices to ensure that data and information systems are optimized based on the following five criteria:

1. *Data and information systems are tailored to the services, processes and employees.*
In order to carry out a process, information is required. Information systems are needed in order to meet these information needs. The aspects of the information systems that need to be changed in order to properly support the (future) processes must be made clear.

It must also be possible to control processes. Naturally, information is also needed in order to carry out governing processes. Separate information systems are available for this, such as a data warehouse (DWH). It must be clear how to achieve proper support for the (future) governing processes.

Support for employees in the execution of their work activities is going further and further. Applications are being used to fully automate increasingly large portions of processes.

The era in which an organization's information systems are only directly accessible for its employees is now long gone. Nowadays we have websites, self-service portals, online stores and bank apps. An organization has choices to make regarding which digital media will be offered in addition to, or in place of non-digital media (incidentally, making these choices is part of the Customers & Services aspect). This is neither limited to only (potential) customers, nor to just consumers. The same also applies for suppliers, business partners and other stakeholders.

In addition to externally accessible information systems, an organization must also make choices regarding which applications they want to use for communication with the outside world. This ranges from interactive voice response systems to applications which customers use to chat with call center staff.

Support is also required in the form of applications for communication between employees. Employees want to be able to use the tools they find useful for communicating and sharing knowledge outside of their professional lives (such as private social networks, wikis and chat). This trend relates to new ways of organizing work as well as trends in the nature of the work activities themselves. We must determine which communication systems are needed to support the future methods of collaboration.

Aside from applications that support communication, we also have all kinds of applications that can boost productivity in (knowledge-related) work. Generic office automation such as office suites are ubiquitous. However, in addition to these, we also have special productivity applications. Some examples here might be statistical applications and applications to perform simulations. It is necessary to determine which specific roles or capabilities require a boost in productivity (incidentally, determining this is part of the Processes & Organization aspect).

2. It becomes possible to satisfy the increasing demands that customers are placing on services.
Customers are placing more and more demands on services from organizations. These higher demands translate into increased demands on the processes and methods of organizations. They also translate indirectly into higher demands on data and information systems. In contrast, IT (not coincidentally) provides a range of options for meeting these ever increasing demands, and plays a key role in innovation. Aside from the functional requirements on data and information systems, non-functional requirements such as performance and scalability also play a major role. The applications used must also meet the non-functional requirements.

3. Unnecessary complexity is identified and reduced.
In many organizations, the data and information systems are more complicated than necessary. This is often the consequence of inadequate attention to maintenance, failure to successfully integrate the systems of acquired organizations and an inability to work with architectures. As a consequence, it is important to gain an insight into any unjustifiable complexity in data and information systems.

4. It becomes possible to make choices from the available technology.
The number of available technologies is enormous and the technology is ever increasing in power, which means more and more opportunities for innovation. Organizations are faced with the question of which technologies they should and shouldn't use. Important choices must be made because resources are scarce and the capacity for change is limited.

5. The basis for defining infrastructure requirements is clarified.
The design choices made in the areas of automated information systems and communications facilities have consequences in terms of which infrastructure is required. The non-functional requirements such as performance and scalability play a key role here.

In practice, in order to gain a clear picture of the necessary design choices for data and information systems, experience has shown it is wise to design the following three sub-aspects in relation to one another:
1. The information needs of processes. (See subsection 3.4.2.)
2. The ideal demarcation of information domains. (See subsection 3.4.3.)
3. The physical content of information domains with applications and their interrelationships. (See subsection 3.4.4.)

3.4.2   Information systems provide the information needed to execute and control processes

Information is required for the execution and control of processes. These information needs are addressed through the use of information systems. An insight into the information needs (and the processes) is therefore necessary in order to gain a proper understanding of which information systems an organization actually needs. This is even more important if an organization is dealing with changes that could have a major influence on data and information systems. In addition to this, an insight into your information needs can improve your understanding of problems in the organization's data management. These may arise from misunderstandings or because the management of data is not clearly organized.

It is possible to identify the information needs for every process. In addition to the primary internal processes, in some cases it is also the information needs of the governing processes that are relevant. This is particularly the case if the purpose of the business transformation planning is concerned with governance issues and a need exists for greater insight into the required governance information.

In order to identify the information needs, we need to discover the 'topics of discussion'. What does one talk about when executing a particular process? What does one want to know in order to carry out the process? These 'topics of discussion' are known as business objects. They are 'things' whose characteristics we want to record, use and manage in the form of data. These 'things' may be physical objects that you can point to, such as buildings, people or products, as well as abstract objects, such as insurance policies, organizations or claims. Objects may also be events, such as a wedding, a delivery or a departure.

In order to gain a structured overview of the objects whose properties we want to record in the form of data, we can use a business object model. The purpose of a business object model is to define the objects, understand how the business objects interrelate and identify the main properties of these objects. (Figure 3.14 shows an example of a business object model.)

The CUSTOMER business object, for instance, could be defined as follows in terms of the PRODUCT and CLAIM objects: 'A CUSTOMER is a natural person that purchases or will purchase a PRODUCT from our organization, which gives rise to a CLAIM.' The PRODUCT and CLAIM objects can then be defined as well.

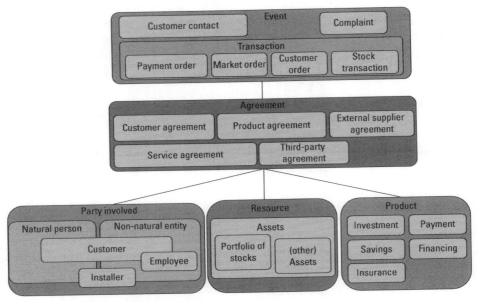

Figure 3.14   Example of a business object model

A general bank had acquired a private bank with the aim of integrating it into its own services. The business transformation plan was about mapping out the consequences of this integration.

A business object model was used as a tool to gain insight, involving representatives from both banks, into the extent to which they had different viewpoints of the 'things' for which data was recorded. For instance, they examined the extent to which concepts such as customer, product and agreement differed from one another. Drafting a business object model was a quick way to pinpoint potential integration problems in the area of data management. Doing this with representatives from both banks enhanced everyone's understanding of the similarities and differences between the two parties.

It is also possible to use a model from data modeling, such as an Entity Relationship Diagram (ERD). When choosing a method of describing data, it is important to bear in mind the purpose of the model. Typically, not much detail is required, it is more about establishing the key objects along with their main properties. A business object model is the best suited for this. This is because it does not need to be an information system design!

3.4.3 Future-proof choices for the design of data and information systems are based on an ideal demarcation of information domains

Suppose we have just mapped out the end-to-end processes for an organization (in general terms). Then let us further suppose that we have also mapped out the information needs for these processes (in general terms). We can now ask which information systems should ideally be implemented in order to provide for the information needs of these processes. This issue is about an optimal demarcation of the information systems of an organization. Optimal demarcation of information systems ensures flexibility in processes and information systems on the one hand, and, on the other hand, cohesion and uniformity between processes and information systems.

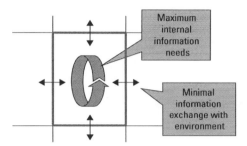

Figure 3.15   Tight cohesion and loose coupling

As detailed in subsection 3.4.2, the information needs are mapped out based on the business objects. Processes receive their information using data that represents the properties of these business objects. However, processes also give rise to new data on business objects that must be recorded. Information systems manage cohesive clusters of data for processes relating to availability across time and space (time: the data that we record today will also be needed tomorrow; space: we may need the data at different physical locations). In this process, it is desirable to identify clusters of processes with strong interrelationships in terms of information needs and weak external information exchanges (loose coupling and tight cohesion). Clusters of this kind are also called 'information domains' or 'logical information systems' (Stoop & Silvius, 2013).

We distinguish two techniques that can help identify information domains:
1. *Use of the business capability model as a starting point for the (logical) information systems architecture.*
   Capabilities are also logically demarcated clusters of activities, people and resources. In data processing organizations, this demarcation logically has a lot to do with the data processing that must be performed in a capability. That is why this is a good starting point to identify an information domain for each capability.
2. *Drafting a CU or CRUD matrix.*
   We can also use a matrix to plot out processes against their data processing. This is known as a CU or CRUD matrix. The letters C and U stand for Create and Use and CRUD stands for Create, Read, Update & Delete. These matrices have work processes or process steps along the vertical axis and business objects or entities on the horizontal axis. Next,

in the cells of this matrix, you enter the actions (C or U or C, R, U or D) that the relevant work process or process step will carry out on the business object or entity in question. We can shift the columns and rows of the matrix to look for clusters of high cohesion in a group of work processes or process steps on the one hand and a group of business objects or entities on the other. A cluster of this kind represents an information domain.

In practice, it appears that it is more difficult to get good results with the second technique than it is with the first. For this reason, the second technique tends to be used in a supplemental way, if needed, to streamline discussions on demarcation.

Whichever technique is selected, ultimately the aim is to achieve a proper understanding of the value that the organization adds, the parts into which it can be divided and the resulting information needs. Drafting a (logical) information systems architecture is a creative process involving the advisor (core team member), specialists in the organization (such as business transformation analysts, architects, IT specialists) and management.

An organization in the area of asset management drew up a business transformation plan covering the years 2012 to 2014. The application landscape was patchy and a clear picture was needed of what the landscape of the future would look like.

Drafting a (logical) information systems architecture ensured that a discussion could take place around data and information systems, separately from the physical content in terms of applications and the unclear application landscape.

Once agreement had been reached on the (logical) information systems architecture, it was time to start outlining the two possible scenarios for the physical content of the (logical) information systems architecture in 2020, separately from the question of which specific application would be used for this. This clarified the key choices that needed to be made. One point on which the scenarios differed was the applications to be used for trading and settlement: should they opt for multiple applications to handle both trading and settlement for specific financial instruments, or individual applications targeted specifically at either trading or settlement? Based on the physical content of the (logical) information systems architecture for 2014, it became clear which step should be taken initially.

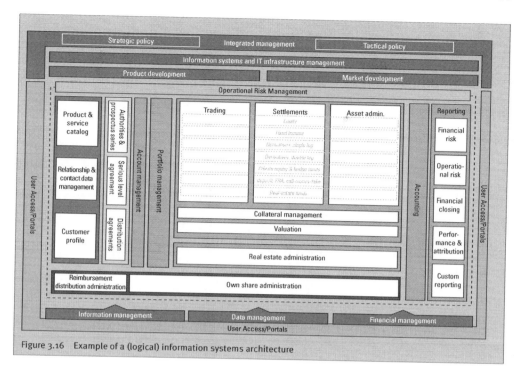

Figure 3.16   Example of a (logical) information systems architecture

The (logical) information systems architecture is a vital tool for aligning the running of a business with data and information systems. This is the step to get to the functionality and information required to carry out the processes. The (logical) information systems architecture offers a holistic overview of the required data and information systems, separately from their physical contents with applications. In practice, this is a highly useful intermediary step. People often tend to think in terms of the current application landscape. The (logical) information systems architecture helps you to take a step back, discuss application boundaries and think in terms of scenarios.

It is extremely helpful to use the (logical) information systems architecture (which can often fit on just one sheet of A4 paper) as a stepping-stone. The current applications and those in development, the data flows, the responsibilities for information domains, the current constraints: all examples of items that can be 'plotted' on the (logical) information systems architecture.

3.4.4   The application landscape and the desired functionality of the data and information systems

Previously, we went into detail on the information needs and optimal demarcation of the information domains. Applications provide the physical content for all, or part, of one or more information domains. An application is a collection of automated and related functionalities, along with the data managed by these functionalities, with its own planning for new versions, releases and modifications.

An organization can develop applications itself, but more typically they will purchase them. The set of all applications is commonly referred to as the application landscape.

The question we can ask now is what the desired application landscape should look like. The (logical) information systems architecture described in the preceding subsection is a useful tool for answering this question. If we were to build the application landscape from the ground up and optimize it for cohesion and flexibility, it would consist of application module(s), each covering a single information domain. In this case, the application landscape looks the same as the (logical) information systems architecture. However, in practice, the current application landscape is almost always the starting point, so commencing from the ground up is not really an option. In addition to this, cohesion and flexibility are actually just two of many angles of approach.

Thus, in practice, most application landscapes do not match the (logical) information systems architecture for and there may be very good reasons for this. Other considerations apart from cohesion and flexibility also play a role, such as the availability of software packages for specific information domains, the effort needed to interface different applications and the costs of the various separate applications compared to a single integrated application. For instance, an organization may consciously opt to use a single ERP (Enterprise Resource Planning) package to cover multiple information domains.

That is why we start by plotting the current application landscape on the (logical) information systems architecture, since this activity can identify potential constraints. This is because the plot shows the information domains that have not yet been provided for in full, the information domains for which multiple applications (perhaps even partially overlapping ones) are in use and the applications that cross information domain boundaries. The resultant plot raises questions, but we cannot directly deduce from it whether we are dealing with a constraint or an undesired situation for the future. This will require proper discussion because an application landscape will have grown a great deal over the years and the situation (or certain aspects of it) will require careful consideration.

It is also a good idea to compare purchased applications with the (logical) information systems architecture. The modular structure of a purchased application will, preferably, line up with the information domains.

As stated, the current application landscape's 'fit' with the (logical) information systems architecture is just one of many factors for assessing applications. The interrelationships of the applications in the form of links and interfaces are often related to this 'fit'. For instance, a highly fragmented application landscape often results in many interfaces, or even in missing interfaces. It is also possible to gain insight into, and assess, the complexity and completeness of the data exchanges.

In addition to this, applications should also be assessed for quality and costs. The importance of this may sometimes be underestimated, but it becomes immediately clear once we realize that in many organizations, a large amount of the total IT expenditure is spent on basic infrastructure and information systems for secondary processes. Insight into the quality and costs of applications enables effective allocation of scarce resources. This prevents undesirable outcomes, such as investments in applications that are rarely used anymore, applications based on obsolete technologies or applications that have become difficult to maintain (legacy systems). The better an organization acts to prevent inefficient investments in the current application landscape, the more financial resources it can allocate to improvements and modernization. In addition, this also ensures the quality of the current application landscape which, in turn, prevents delays in technology upgrades, etc.

Quality has two sides: functional and technical. Functional quality is related to the importance of the application for the user organization. Technical quality is related to the non-functional aspects of an application, such as maintainability, expandability, fit with the IT architecture and continuity of suppliers of the application and underlying technologies. Here we are entering the area of Application Portfolio Management (APM).

Evaluating the current application landscape can be a time-consuming process. This is especially so if much of the necessary information, such as the cost of applications, is not available. The assessment of the current application landscape can be undertaken with extensive and careful support, but in practice we have also had good experiences with a more pragmatic approach in which process and system owners, architects and managers have been asked for their professional estimates of the criteria. This bridges the gap between attempts at expressing the quality of applications, which are often made separately from one another. In this way, this approach contributes to the discussion of the extent to which applications do or do not provide value.

Once we have a clear picture of the current application landscape and its shortcomings, we can start outlining the target application landscape. This raises a number of questions: should we opt for a best-of-breed or best-of-suite strategy? Should we make another large investment in a bespoke application, or opt for a package solution? How do we purge the technologically obsolete applications as quickly as possible? Wherever possible, it is desirable to work these kinds of issues out within the context of the business transformation plan. If this is not possible, then define an action item to conduct a preliminary study, with this kind of action item perhaps being adopted as a regular project.

The (logical) information systems architecture allows you to compare different scenarios for a future application landscape with their pros and cons. If there is a major difference between the current and future application landscapes, then it may be necessary to define different plateaus to represent the migration over time. For instance, an application landscape for each year in the planning period.

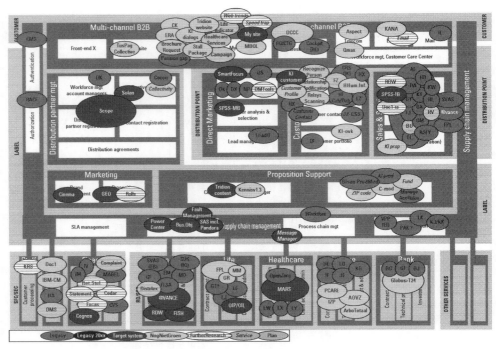

Figure 3.17   Example of an application landscape on a logical information systems architecture

3.5   IT Infrastructure & Facilities: despite standardization and outsourcing, there are key decisions to be made

In order to use technical resources, the user does not typically need to know exactly how the technology behind it works. You can drive a car without knowing exactly how everything works, you can heat up food in the microwave with no knowledge of electromagnetic radiation and you can process text or surf the web without knowing exactly how a computer works. Good thing! However, there are choices that the user will in fact need to make hat will have consequences on the underlying technology. Sometimes there are considerations to weigh between the different user requirements or between the current set of requirements and the future possibilities based on new technologies. If you buy a car then you need to decide, for instance, whether you should go for sporty, or economical. A fancy sports car requires different technology, but also normally comes at a higher price. In addition, a sports car might well limit future possibilities, because it will not be particularly well suited to serve as a family car. In short, technology does indeed have an impact because the choices must always take into account the current and future possibilities for use as well as associated risks and costs.

Section 3.4 considered the question of how to use information systems to provide optimal support for the services, processes and organization. In turn, the design choices made in the area of automated information and communication systems also have consequences on the IT Infrastructure & Facilities required. Section 3.3 on the Processes & Organization aspect has already mentioned that the desired method of organization also influences the IT Infrastructure & Facilities aspect.

For most managers and employees, only part of the IT Infrastructure & Facilities are visible. They may work with an application on a desktop, for instance. In the background, an array of network components, system software and hardware are necessary to provide the functionality that is visible to the user. (See Figure 3.18.)

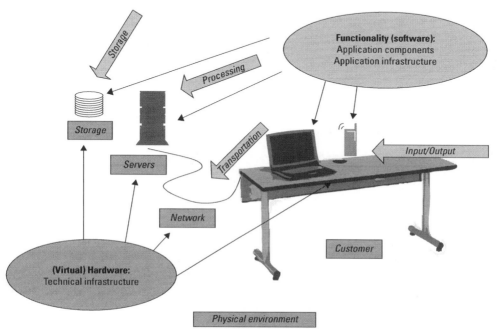

Figure 3.18   'Invisible' IT Infrastructure & Facilities

For all infrastructure and (shared) facilities it is true that once is they are in place, working properly, dimensioned properly and the financing is in order (including the maintenance costs), we can use things without thinking about them. However, this does not happen on its own: it is the result of a targeted process and a targeted design. Another factor is that with certain IT infrastructure choices, an organization commits itself for a longer period of time due to the impact and costs involved (such as for hosting infrastructure in an external data center).

That is why the IT Infrastructure & Facilities aspect is just as critical from a business perspective. It is essential to have proper insight into the design of the infrastructure and the choices you make to support or enable the target organization. Despite a great deal of standardization and increased outsourcing of IT Infrastructure & Facilities, an organization still has key considerations to weigh up from both strategic and operational perspectives. Ideally, based on design choices, the following points will become clear:

1. *Make it clear how the organization deals with the sourcing of IT Infrastructure & Facilities, including management.*
One key choice that every organization must make in terms of IT Infrastructure & Facilities is between DIY (Do It Yourself) and outsourcing. This does not have to be an all-or-nothing choice: it can be different for different infrastructure components. For instance, an organization must choose whether to use its own internal or external data center or a third-party data center. Here, we also have the choice of whether you want to be the owner of the IT infrastructure or if you want to rent, lease or use a pay-per-use arrangement. The field of infrastructure has seen turbulent trends in recent years (such as the cloud, mobile and BYOD (Bring Your Own Device)), which are compelling many organizations to rethink their sourcing for infrastructure (and applications). The choice that is made will have implications for different types of management activities. Outsourcing often has benefits in terms of costs, technical knowledge and skills but it is not without its drawbacks. For example, it requires the competency to effectively manage an outsourcing partner (direction). Content-based IT knowledge is still indispensable for this. An organization usually gives up some flexibility, but professionalization can facilitate the enforcement of policies, such as standardization.

2. *Make it clear how the required IT capacity will be available at the right time and to an adequate degree.*
IT capacity is about processing capacity, storage capacity and network bandwidth. Many may take the approach: 'work out what you need and look for the cheapest supplier'. Unfortunately, it is not that simple, it's rarely the case that an organization needs the same amount of IT capacity at all hours of the day and for every day of the year. This means we are dealing with highs and lows. In addition to this, we must take into account future trends in operational management. However, IT infrastructure is often purchased or acquired based on the expected peak load, taking into account a certain margin for exceptions. It is precisely on this point that a business must make choices.

For instance, it is possible in some cases to distribute the load of the IT infrastructure more evenly over the day or year. One example here would be insurance providers. One business choice may be to renew all policies on January 1st which will likely result in an enormous peak load. An alternative might be to have insurance policies renew annually on the dates on which they were first taken out. This gives a much more even demand for capacity over the year. Of course, this has its limitations. All health insurance policies are required by Dutch law to renew on January 1st. Another possible alternative would be to make the infrastructure scalable and purchase it on a pay-per-use basis. This is clearly related to the sourcing of the IT Infrastructure & Facilities. One implication of this, however, is that the costs become much more variable (i.e. less predictable). Consequently, the cash flow must be able to absorb this variability. In addition to this, the business case must be based on a representative consumption pattern, otherwise, the organization may be in for some surprises. It must be clear how an organization will anticipate this.

3. *Make it clear which risks an organization is prepared to accept regarding continuity and information security.*

If an organization wants to reduce risks in areas such as hacking, system failure, fire, etc. to a minimum, this will have major consequences on costs and investments on the one hand, and ease-of-use on the other. Therefore, in addition to the requirements that must be adhered to in relation to legislation, the business management of an organization must also carefully consider how much risk is deemed to be acceptable. As part of this process, they must weigh the consequences of the risk actually occurring against the costs and efforts associated in ensuring that the IT facilities are constantly available for use by employees and customers. This touches on topics such as information security, data recovery and business continuity planning.

One good example here is online banking from a smartphone. In many cases, the necessary transactions can be made with a low level of security (much lower than for banking on a PC). The trade-off here is that transferring funds from a phone requires a certain degree of ease-of-use in order for customers to actually use the facility. Incidentally, part of the choice lies with the customers themselves, who determine the maximum transfer sum for banking by phone.

One tool used to classify risks here is the CIA classification (Confidentiality, Integrity and Availability). We can then set appropriate measures for the different risk classifications.

4. *Make it clear what standards an organization has chosen and how to ensure adherence to these.*

Standardization of an IT infrastructure typically has a positive effect on costs (through acquisition, management and use). Some examples here would be standardization in the area of hardware, operating systems, middleware, mobile phones and data exchange. But standardization must be actively enforced because morbid growth is always afoot. One approach is to establish a corporate policy in the area of infrastructure and ensure adherence to it. Several considerations are relevant to the business here. One of the choices involves what should be standardized in a centralized manner and where a greater degree of freedom will be permitted in a decentralized manner. However, it may make sense to agree on a standard for newly developed applications or components. Business must make these decisions. For some types of organizations, the choice of software packages is far from overwhelming. Therefore, in this case, the likelihood of a package meeting the organization's standards is much lower. The organization must use a proper cost/benefit analysis to make a choice between the functional benefits and technical and cost-related drawbacks. One special category here is what is known as application infrastructure. This concerns standard platforms for implementing management information, Internet portals, content management, process control, integration/interfaces, etc. An approach frequently taken is to select a generic application infrastructure for the entire organization that is used to give different organizational units the freedom to implement their own solutions.

5. *Make it clear which IT facilities employees will receive.*
A great deal is changing in the area of IT facilities for employees. They are now familiar with technology that is more advanced and often more user-friendly than that which they receive from their employer to perform their work. New generations of employees expect to be able to work independently of time and place. Flexible workstations are actually the standard in newly designed office environments. Employees are increasingly being given freedom of choice in the tools they want to use. One example here is the concept of Bring Your Own Device (BYOD), which lets employees use their own laptops, phones and tablets to do their work. All of this requires a clear policy from the organization, in which they must carefully weigh up user convenience against information security risks, manageability and associated infrastructure investments and costs.

6. *Make it clear how the costs of the IT Infrastructure & Facilities will be shared across the organization.*
A feature of IT Infrastructure & Facilities is that the facilities are usually used by multiple applications, are vital to different organizational units and are required for multiple initiatives (incidentally, this also applies to generic applications such as office automation, ERP packages and data warehouses). However, this raises the question of whether the initial investments and the ongoing operating costs should be covered by all of the different users. An organization has various options here. For instance, it can finance all IT infrastructure at the organizational level and include it in the general charges. This makes charging costs simpler and creates transparency regarding who must pay for the investments and costs. This model ensures that the entire organization helps pay for the facilities (whether or not an organizational unit actually uses them) and requires strict governance on the acquisition and/or commissioning of new infrastructure. At the other end of the spectrum, we have a decentralized model where organizational units or projects themselves must cover the investment and operating costs for new IT infrastructure. However, this may result in infrastructure going unpurchased, when from an organizational perspective it is actually justified. One consequence of this, for instance, may be that in the absence of the infrastructure, more 'creative' solutions are found, such as building your own application infrastructure, even when it is readily available on the market.

Another challenge is that many projects often prefer not to involve the complexity of new generic infrastructure because it inflates the scope. For instance, other organizational units may want to have an input into the decision-making on the requirements. For this reason, it is often more convenient to implement generic infrastructure as a separate project. Here, we must clearly indicate what the project is a precondition for, to prevent it from being seen as merely a cost item.

7. Provide insight into what must change in terms of IT Infrastructure & Facilities in order to support or enable the target organization.

The above aspects set out the requirements for the IT Infrastructure & Facilities. It is necessary to gain insight into the significance of the intended organizational approach to IT infrastructure that is adopted from the options outlined above. But the strategy may also have a direct impact on the infrastructure landscape, as in the case of an organization-wide objective to reduce costs. It is vital here to determine the extent to which fundamental changes in the infrastructure landscape are needed or if it is 'more (or less) of the same'. Rethinking the sourcing may also involve this kind of fundamental change. However, in this context, it is also important to look at new technological developments and trends which can offer opportunities for the organization. Previously (in section 3.1), we referred to this as 'enabling'. There is no shortage of examples of technology trends: the cloud, big data, mobility, etc.

But how do we get a good picture of the target design for the IT Infrastructure & Facilities? For this, we will start with a definition of what we understand by the term 'IT Infrastructure & Facilities'. Next, we will discuss the use of a logical model and other models in making design choices. Finally, we will cover the remaining design choices. In addition, as far as the IT Infrastructure & Facilities aspect is concerned, conscious choices must be made regarding what the business transformation plan should focus on. The design choices mentioned above can be used as a guideline here.

3.5.1 A (logical) model helps provide insight into the current and target infrastructure landscapes

IT Infrastructure & Facilities can be subdivided into:

1. Application infrastructure: basic software products on which application components run, or on which application components can be implemented. Here, we draw a distinction between operating systems, application servers (generic application platforms that are built on top of an operating system) and generic business servers (such as portal servers, workflow management systems and Business Process Management systems).

2. Technical infrastructure: this comprises all hardware, peripherals and other equipment such as servers, hard drives, printers, plotters, monitors, PCs, laptops, landline phones, smartphones and networks including smart components such as routers and switches. Here, we define 'networks' as facilities for data transfer between two or more devices.

3. Technical structure of software: applications consist of application components: computer programs and parts thereof that provide one or more services. Here, we distinguish between:

    a. Interaction services: support the interaction of employees, customers and other organizations.

    b. Control services: handle transfer of cases between different organizations (choreography) or capabilities (Business Process Management or orchestration), or support for process step completion by employees (computer-assisted case handling or workflow management).

c. Processing or data services: performance of specific work activities, such as saving business data, retrieval of business data, retrieval of data sets, performance of checks, compilation of data into documents and other forms of transferable information.
d. Infrastructure services: such as file and print services, record management services, identity management services, logging services, network services, messaging services, firewall services, backup & recovery services and transformation services. This latter category also includes:
   • Services provided by application suites called Enterprise Service Buses (ESBs);
   • Physical locations where IT Infrastructure & Facilities are accommodated, e.g. data center sites, including corresponding physical facilities such as cabling, phone lines, fiber-optics and air conditioning systems.

A distinction can also be made between:
• IT Infrastructure & Facilities for end users of business applications;
• IT Infrastructure & Facilities specifically for developers and managers of applications, application components and infrastructure components.

Some examples of the latter would be monitoring tools, software distribution facilities, development centers and backup software. Facilities for (information) security, such as authentication and authorization tools and antivirus software may also be distinguished separately.

Applications that are visible and recognizable to end users or other users are included under the Information & Applications aspect. The IT Infrastructure & Facilities aspect includes everything 'in the background' together with applications specifically for people like software developers and managers.

The components mentioned above are visualized in a logical model for IT Infrastructure & Facilities. This provides a static view of the components of the infrastructure which possibly (or definitely) will be needed. It is important to select a logical model that links up with the organization and the focus and objectives of the business transformation project. Models already in use in the organization's IT department are typically preferred.

Figure 3.19 shows an example of a logical model.

After a choice has been made for a particular logical model, it can then be used to plot the current physical infrastructure. The logical model can also be used to plot any constraints or opportunities for improvement.

Figure 3.20 plots the current physical infrastructure onto the logical model.

What can we do with a logical model and the physical components plotted on it?
1. Show what physical infrastructure is present for each component in the logical model. This may identify some interesting points, for instance that the organization is currently

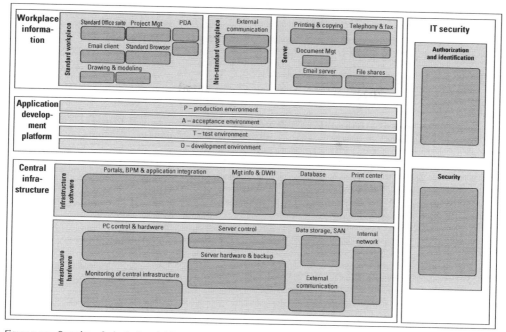

Figure 3.19   Overview of a logical model for IT Infrastructure & Facilities

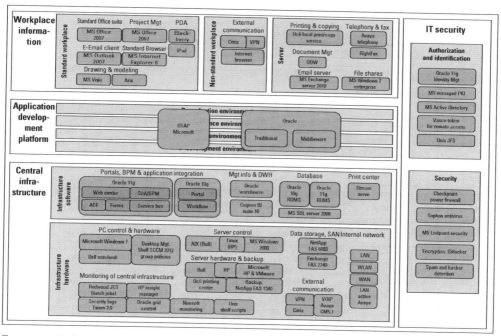

Figure 3.20   IT Infrastructure & Facilities depicted using the logical model

using three different kinds of databases. Also if an organization has multiple physical locations where infrastructure is in use, any duplication in infrastructure may be invisible. This may raise the question of how much more standardization is sensible and feasible. In addition to this, the lack of physical components for a particular logical component may also raise questions.

2. Serve as a tool for looking at the sourcing of the infrastructure landscape or its parts. Here, it may be useful to go into detail in terms of what type of infrastructure is present at different locations in the organization and which management regimes apply to different parts of the infrastructure.

3. Serve as a tool for determining, in a structured way, what changes are needed in the infrastructure landscape to support or enable the target organization. Here, we may think about new types of infrastructure components that are necessary in the landscape, such as tablets, a portal server or a 3D printer. It may also mean that adjustments are necessary in terms of IT capacity, such as greater flexibility in scaling processing capacities up/down.

It is often the case that 'work' is performed at different locations within an organization. This is true, for instance, in the case of a central head office and decentralized branches or stores, or in the case of distribution centers. In such instances it is normally desirable for this to be reflected in the infrastructure models. This is especially true when a particular infrastructure is specific to a particular kind of location, when constraints are specific to particular kinds of locations, or simply when changes occur in the locations where 'work' will be performed. For each location, we can then plot the physical infrastructure onto the logical model. However, the interrelationships between the different types of locations may also be of interest. The example below describes a logical model for an organization with multiple locations interconnected with the head office in different ways.

A general bank had acquired a private bank with the aim of integrating it into its own services. The business transformation plan was concerned with mapping out the consequences of this integration.

The IT Infrastructure & Facilities aspect started with mapping out – in a structured way – the IT Infrastructure & Facilities used in the private bank. Based on a logical model of the IT Infrastructure & Facilities used in the general bank, the physical components in the private bank were then mapped out. This inventory quickly pinpointed any potential integration issues. The structured examination provided a complete holistic overview of all deviating IT Infrastructure & Facilities. The conclusion was that there were only a small number of integration issues. One of the differences involved the use of voice logging (logging phone calls). In the private bank, all phone calls, both internal and external, were voice-logged, the threshold for monitoring a call was low and the costs of the service were spread across the organization as general IT costs. This was not the case in the general bank.

As mentioned in the introduction, there are still some design choices which may be relevant and that we can focus on in further detail.

Depending on the scope, a reconsideration of the sourcing of components for the infrastructure landscape and/or their management may be major issues. An integral weighing of the different factors (including business factors) is vital here. Some of the factors to bear in mind include the consequences on the cost structure and finance, staff, privacy, integration, flexibility and the extent to which any necessary direction role can be fulfilled. Therefore, in addition to infrastructure specialists, you must also bring in specialists from other fields. If specialist expertise is not adequately available in the organization, then it is advisable to rely on external expertise.

Business continuity and information security are broad areas of study. They range from failover facilities to privacy aspects for customer data stored 'somewhere in the cloud'. These two topics may result not only in specific infrastructure requirements (such as SIEM: Security Information & Event Management) but also in requirements in the area of certification of data centers, staff or applications. There may also be a requirement to deploy specialists in the areas of Business Continuity Management (BCM) and information security.

The manner in which the costs of the IT Infrastructure & Facilities are distributed across the organization can have numerous consequences on how to deal with this in practice. One wants to achieve an allocation of costs that results in effective and efficient deployment along with the effective and efficient use of the IT Infrastructure & Facilities. However, this is not so easy to achieve. One must carefully consider the consequences of a particular cost allocation model and it is normally necessary to take compensatory measures for any drawbacks and risks. A controller is indispensable in discussions on this topic.

Setting standards is one thing, but we must also ensure adherence to these standards. One or more mechanisms must be in place to guarantee this. Some examples here would be a properly functioning enterprise architecture function and a well-designed supply/demand organization.

3.6   Summary

This chapter has focused on the horizontal interrelationships in the BTF. The framework distinguishes between four aspects of running an organization: Customers & Services, Processes & Organization, Information & Applications and IT Infrastructure & Facilities. The framework represents these aspects as columns. These aspects must be analyzed and designed separately, as well as in relation to one another. This is the only way to make the transition or 'translation' from strategy and objectives to the business transformation portfolio, where completeness and consistency are achieved in the areas of guiding principles, design choices and action items.

We have noted that for each business transformation plan, conscious choices must be made on where the focus should lie. For each aspect, you should identify the most relevant points to be worked out with regard to the situation at hand. For each aspect, we have provided some basic guidance to help make the best choices in each situation.

For the Customers & Services aspect, we have explained that it is a good idea to design four sub-aspects in relation to one another: markets & customer segments, products & services, the distribution channels and the customer contacts & media.

Under the Processes & Organization aspect, we discussed the 'work' to be performed in order to provide added-value to the customer. A process model and a business capability model were described as tools for analyzing the design of the work. Next, we proceeded to an organization model, before concluding with a discussion of governance.

The Information & Applications aspect covers three sub-aspects of data and information systems. First, we addressed the information needed to execute and control processes. Next, we went into detail with regard to the logical demarcation of the data and information systems based on the (logical) information systems architecture. Finally, we looked at the application landscape in relation to the (logical) information systems architecture.

We then moved on to the IT Infrastructure & Facilities aspect. The infrastructure landscape is structured using a logical model and this can be filled with current or target physical components in order to gain insight into several areas. Finally, we focused on some necessary design choices related to the infrastructure landscape.

4 A good planning process paves the way for successful organizational change

People want to change, but do not like to be changed. When drafting the business transformation plan, therefore, it is essential to involve stakeholders and assign responsibilities to them for the desired organizational improvement. It is an investment of time, money and people that more than pays for itself in the form of: higher quality, better and more creative design choices, a supportive base, more energy, less resistance, mutual understanding and cooperation. These matters contribute to an easier, smoother and more elegant implementation of organizational improvement.

In practice, what often occurs is that a business transformation plan created in a back room by a small group of professionals amounts to little or no actual change. Therefore, we must plan organizational improvement well. We must ensure that the stakeholders themselves want the change, and also that the organization can deliver it. Working out and implementing organizational improvements sometimes requires new or different disciplines from an organization, or simply more capacity in the same disciplines. (See also section 5.1.) In other cases, the organization and governance of improvement projects is not in order, or is not even fully designed. However, nothing is quite so frustrating as having a good business transformation plan and a unanimous willingness to execute it, but not knowing where to start, how to approach it, who should undertake it or how to manage all of the improvement projects. Often, this is not necessary either. It takes between one to three months to complete a business transformation planning project. During the preparation of the business transformation plan, this time would be well spent building up or reinforcing the necessary disciplines and getting their governance in order.

Of course, the lead time for a business transformation planning project is not sufficient for this, but it *can* be used to set things in motion. In this case, when planning the business transformation portfolio, it is necessary to take into account a limited but increasing capacity for change in the organization. Therefore, it is vital to prepare a plan with suitable content, bring in and assign responsibility to the right people and also ensure that the organization has the right disciplines in-house for the transformation.

In many situations, however, other factors are at play. For instance, consider limiting factors such as organizational culture, unhealthy relationship patterns or a counterproductive organizational structures. These are often major obstacles to getting an organizational change off the ground.

Other examples of obstacles to organizational change are: responsibility-avoiding culture, lack of fixed-role behavior, dependent personnel relationships or payroll structures that promote counterproductive behavior. For successful organizational change, it is critical to identify these issues when drafting the business transformation plan, address them where possible and take measures against them. This does in fact require the necessary change management expertise and experience. Thus, after chapters 2 and 3, the reader may have the impression that the challenge in making a business transformation plan lies primarily in its content. In this chapter, we will explain why that is not the case. To conclude, we can say that when implementing a business transformation planning project, we are working to achieve results at four levels in order to ultimately achieve organizational improvements:

1. Design: first off, we work to define structured organizational improvements and create an actual business transformation plan. This involves designing and planning the intended transformation using the framework described in chapters 2 and 3.
2. Willingness: second, we ensure that stakeholders take responsibility for the planned business transformation. We primarily do this by intensively involving stakeholders in the design and planning of the organizational change.
3. Ability: the third level is concerned with building up and reinforcing the organization's capacity for improvement by continuing to work on the required disciplines, the required capacity, or the effective organization and governance of improvement projects.
4. Conditioning: finally, interventions are often necessary in order to ensure, for instance, that limiting factors such as organizational culture, unhealthy relationship patterns or counterproductive structures are identified, addressed, mitigated or directly removed.

In the rest of this chapter, we will discuss the first three levels. Level 4 is not specific to the BTF. A variety of change management literature is available to consult on this topic.

When drafting a business transformation plan, the activities are performed in three phases: the initiation phase, the development phase and the delivery phase. (See Figure 4.1.) Each phase has a clear goal and consists of several steps. In each phase, activities are conducted and results recorded for all of the first three levels.

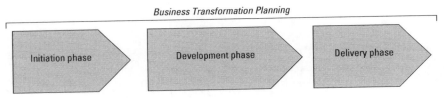

Business Transformation Planning

Initiation phase   Development phase   Delivery phase

Figure 4.1   Planning process phases

The initiation phase serves to prepare an organization for the optimal completion of the next two phases of formulating the business transformation plan. In addition to this, the initiation phase also examines the degree to which the organization is, or appears to have been, able to implement changes and which improvements are required here (level 3 - ability). In the development phase, the plan is actually drawn up. The delivery phase ensures that all results that have been achieved in drafting the business transformation plan are put to optimal use within the organization.

Business transformation planning always goes through these three phases. The content of these phases is, however, always different. Each business transformation planning project has unique motivations, strives towards different objectives and exists in a different context, a different organization and its own unique point in time. That is why the approach is never exactly the same.

All three phases are indispensable in a good business transformation planning project and must also be carried out in full, achieving results at all levels. The message here is: do it right or don't do it at all. Go through all the phases, without skipping any steps. Otherwise, there is a good chance it will come to little or nothing in terms of actual organizational improvement, which is a waste of the time, money and energy put into it. In the rest of this chapter, we will discuss the three business transformation planning phases in further detail and explain what needs to be done in each phase at each of the first three levels.

4.1 Initiation must ensure a focused approach that is tailored to the situation

It is often tempting to just skip the initiation phase and get right down to the 'content'. That would be a missed opportunity, because proper preparation is half the battle. Unfortunately, these projects fail all too often because the team wants to start working out the business transformation plan right away, usually with a small group of 'experts' and without careful consideration of the process, let alone the required competencies.

For this reason, we might also call the 'initiation phase' the 'reconnaissance phase'. Although the final result of this phase is an action plan for the development and delivery phases, the initiation phase is about much more than just writing an action plan. It is all about taking a step back, attempting to size up the situation, looking at what is available, what level and pace of change the organization can attain and using all of this to determine what needs to happen in the subsequent phases, which approach is the best fit and what disciplines need to be reinforced or built up. It is precisely the business transformation planners with long histories working in the organization who may fail to see the need for the initiation phase, but this phase is all the more critical for them. It is an effective tool for exposing deeply rooted misconceptions and group-think, to which everyone is susceptible to a certain degree.

As mentioned, results are achieved at different levels in every phase of a business transformation planning project. That includes the initiation phase. Figure 4.2 shows the activities for the initiation phase.

At the level of design, it is important to clarify the underlying motivations and the goals for the plan. A situation outline helps us take a step back from the daily routine and enables a more systematic look at the organization and context. What is the state of the organization? What are the major trends? What is the organization's culture like? How do decisions come about? In addition to this, we also compile an inventory of the resources available. Applying the BTF serves a key function here because it structures all of the available resources and thus clearly shows whether the organization has insight into, or has made choices in regards to,

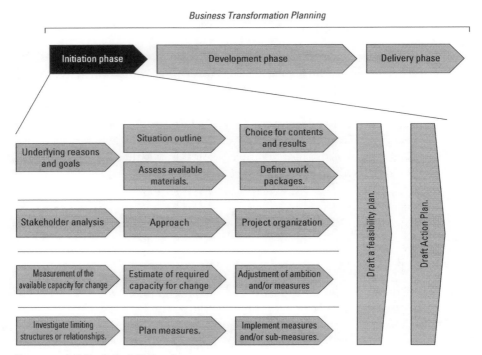

Figure 4.2   Activities in the initiation phase

the different aspects of running an organization as well as how consistent these are with one another. Finally, this results in making scope choices and defining work packages. Moreover, we also conduct a stakeholder analysis. Based on this and on the goals, the situation outline, work packages and scope choices, we can develop an approach and design a project organization.

As early as possible in the initiation phase, we make an estimate of the available capacity for change in the organization. Later on in the initiation phase, once a picture arises of the planned changes in terms of complexity, type of change, scope, etc., we can also prepare an estimate of the required capacity for change. Comparison of the capacity for change available in the organization and the capacity for change needed for the planned transformation results in a number of proposed measures either to increase the capacity for change or adjust ambitions downwards (or perhaps even upwards!).

The steps in the initiation phase do not necessarily need to be performed in a particular order, and sometimes steps are repeated, or overlap with other steps. For instance, in practice we often hold several discussions with the executive to review the underlying motivations as well as the situation, agree the objectives and at a later stage consider a first draft of the approach. Between discussions, we work out the underlying motivations, further investigate the situation and create a first draft for the approach.

4.1.1 Establish the real goals, determine the work to be done and make choices on contents and results

Developing a business transformation plan is also about content components. What is the underlying motivation for the planned change? What are the relevant trends? What is already known and what choices have already been made? Are we making a plan for the next two years or for five years? What do we still need to do to clarify the strategy, map out and analyze the current situation, design the target situation and define the business transformation portfolio? Figure 4.3 shows the activities that are performed at the plan level in the initiation phase.

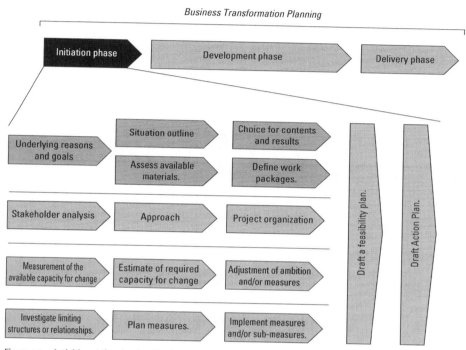

Figure 4.3   Activities at the plan level in the initiation phase

1. *Clear underlying motivations and goals provide a business transformation planning project with focus.*

The first question is: why do we want to deploy a business transformation and what do we want to achieve as an organization? What are our goals? Creating a holistic overview of the underlying reasons will clarify why we are carrying out a business transformation planning project. The underlying reasons may be highly diverse in nature. In practice, we often come across the following kinds of reasons:

- New or adjusted strategy;
- New manager, new management team;
- Trends in the sector chain;
- Mergers, acquisitions and reorganizations;
- Introduction of new products or services;

- Cost reductions;
- New technology options;
- Innovation of product, process, organization;
- Maintenance backlog and/or products, processes or data and information systems that have grown overly complex;
- Business and IT do not link up with each other;
- Desire for a more long-term vision;
- Large number of constraints in the organization.

If the underlying reasons are acute, then it will be easier to identify goals. Some goals could be:
- Specific action plan to implement the new strategy in the organization within a period of three to five years;
- Improve business/IT alignment, both between processes and systems and between the IT department and the other business units;
- Develop structural solutions for the various constraints already identified;
- Design all of the changes needed to enable introduction of a new product and implement these in processes, systems and infrastructure.

2. *Drawing up an outline situation is always enlightening.*
In addition to a preparing an overview of the underlying motivations, we also map out the situation. This is because we will take a contingency approach to determining the approach for a business transformation planning project. This means both the content and the way of working is determined based on the characteristics of the specific situation in which the business transformation planning project will be executed. Therefore, it is necessary to analyze the situation properly. When preparing a situation outline, we always examine:
- The scope, complexity and culture of the organization;
- Developments in the environment of the organization and within the organization itself;
- The ambitions and the level of ambition of the management;
- The presence and clarity of the strategy;
- What the main products/services of the organization are;
- What phase of automation/computerization the organization is in;
- The quality and maturity of the existing process design and control;
- The main strategic and other issues;
- The main constraints or problems;
- Prior experiences with business transformation planning or similar approaches to change;
- Experiences with strategic business transformations and existing governance mechanisms.

3. *We make maximum use of the resources that are available and usable.*
It would be naive to think that in an organization a lot has not already been mapped out, that good choices have not already been made, plans have not already been drawn up, preliminary research has not already been done, etc. A great deal of these activities are often highly useful. This means it is not necessary to reanalyze and redevelop everything. That

would be a waste of time and energy, as well as being disrespectful to the people in the organization who did the work in the first instance.

So, it is important to establish what information is generally available and how useful is it for the business transformation plan? We distinguish several categories here:

- Strategic information refers to everything involved in external or internal strategic analysis, high level objectives such as mission, vision and core values, business models and strategic formulations (the 'how', in general terms), as well as the objectives.
- Other information falls under what we call basic inventory-making. This includes essential information on the current situation, usually the different portfolios, such as:
  - Which products are we actually selling and how many of them are there (product catalog)?
  - How profitable are the various products?
  - What processes are carried out in the organization? What are the key performance indicators? How does the organization score on them? What are the main constraints?
  - How is the organization designed and who works there ('human capital')?
  - What applications are in use, including key features (application portfolio)?
  - What projects are ongoing or already planned (project portfolio)?
- All kinds of analyses that have already been conducted, often due to constraints or developments. One example here would be impact analyses.
- Designs and choices that have been proposed or have already been made. These are often architectures, preliminary research and definition studies.
- Previous change proposals put forward but which may have stalled.
- All manner of financial or other quantitative information that indicates how the organization is performing.

4. Various information collection techniques are employed in the initiation phase.
You can use various methods to research the context, such as interviews, workshops and examining documentation.

- Interviews provide a good opportunity to gage the stakeholder visions and expectations of the business transformation plan. A powerful effect can be achieved by incorporating interview results into the action plan so the interviewees recognize their thoughts and ideas in it. Interviews are often held broadly, with representation from all stakeholder departments, in order to arrive at a picture that is as complete as possible.
- Workshops offer the opportunity to collect high volumes of information quickly or, for instance, to outline the main points of an action plan. It is important to choose a suitable procedure that reflects the target group and situation.
- Examination of existing documentation is intended to provide insight into the situation. Examples of the kinds of documents to be reviewed include strategic plans, annual plans, marketing plans, process descriptions and information strategies and policies. In the initiation phase, the emphasis lies on determining the document's usability, status (is it a formal policy document?) and date. The actual processing of input material is part of the development phase.

5. *Based on the underlying reasons, the goals and a proper understanding of the situation, it is possible to make the necessary scope choices.*
A business transformation plan can be developed for the next two years, or for just one year, or even up to five years. It is possible to work everything out down to the smallest detail, but sometimes a general storyline is all that is needed. Are we working based on specific proposals for improvement, or do we need to work out the strategy in a highly structured manner? Do we look at how to improve the current situation, or do we simply set it aside and focus on more radical steps?

These are crucial questions that require very clear choices from business transformation planners. The choices that can be made for a business transformation plan are (Stoop & Silvius, 2012):

- The scope: is the plan being developed for a chain of organizations, the organization itself or units/departments within the organization? Or would it be preferable to apply a demarcation based on processes, products/services and/or parts of information management?
- The timeframe: is the plan for the short term (one or two years), or does it require a long-term vision (three to five years)? The choice of timeframe is highly dependent on the culture of the organization (are people prepared to set aside the daily routine and look to the future?), the urgency of current constraints and the relative stability of the organization and its environment.
- The level of detail: is the plan worked out in general terms, or do you want a deeper level of detail? Important factors here include the scope and complexity of the organization and the motives. For instance, for an innovation-oriented project, a general definition of new possibilities will suffice, whereas a control and structuring-oriented project may require deeper insight.
- Project mandate: is the plan developed from the top down or the bottom up? The bottom-up approach starts from specific change ideas elicited from the organization and works out solutions for these and plots them in a model with their interrelationships. This model is then tested against the business strategy. The top-down approach takes the business strategy as the starting point, derives guiding principles from it for the new situation and arrives at an action plan by comparing it to the current situation. The choice between top-down and bottom-up is primarily determined by the availability, current relevance and usability of the business strategy and by the degree of decentralization in the organization. A combination of the two approaches is also possible.
- Design focus: do the existing situation and current projects shape the guiding principle (the current situation approach) or are you mainly looking for modernization (target situation approach)? The choice for a current or target situation approach is primarily determined by the quality of the current situation and the management's level of ambition.

6. *Preliminary structuring helps to define the work packages.*
Everyone is familiar with the time boxing phenomenon: a fixed period of time in which a result must be achieved. This allows you to delimit the end result as well. The method for doing this is to pre-structure the business transformation plan by carefully considering

which analyses and architectures must be worked out for each aspect of running a business. This is comparable to developing an outline. In other words, based on underlying reasons, objectives, the situation outline, available resources and scope choice, we determine the components that should make up the business transformation plan and put together work packages based on these.

4.1.2   Map out values and stakeholders, devise an approach and design the project organization

Planning a change using the BTF is the first step in this change! This means that everything that applies to organizational change also applies from day one of the business transformation planning project. It is vital to understand this. Although people often tend to focus on the content, in fact the context and the change process play equally important roles in business transformation projects (Pettigrew & Whipp, 1991). A plan that does not fit the context, is not supported and does not have an owner will have little to no chance of success.

In order to factor in these issues adequately and ensure that the business transformation planning project is used and carried out as a change project, it is necessary to bring in people with knowledge of, and experience in, business transformation projects. It is also important to ensure that the business transformation plan is ultimately supported and the organization wants to implement the change, so it is vital to involve the right stakeholders during the process, emphasizing the urgency for change (or offering perspective) and communicating appropriately throughout the entire project.

In general, different stakeholders have different expectations with regard to the business transformation plan. These values may diverge considerably. The business transformation planning project team will hold discussions with the main stakeholders for two reasons: on the one hand, to put together an inventory of the changes and to define the objectives of the business transformation plan, and on the other hand to conduct expectation management so it is clear exactly which issues the plan will and will not address. Figure 4.4 shows the activities at the level of 'willingness to change'.

We can devise an approach based on the stakeholder analysis in combination with the objectives, the situation outline, scope choices and work packages. Therefore, it is crucial to:
• Have a clear and complete picture of all stakeholders and their values;
• Have a clear picture of the base of support and readiness for change;
• Know who the opinion leaders are and who can contribute.

When designing the project organization, we must ensure that all values are adequately represented.

Conscious choice for approach and organization
In determining the approach to the business transformation planning project, choices need to be made regarding the approach and procedure. The choices you make will be highly

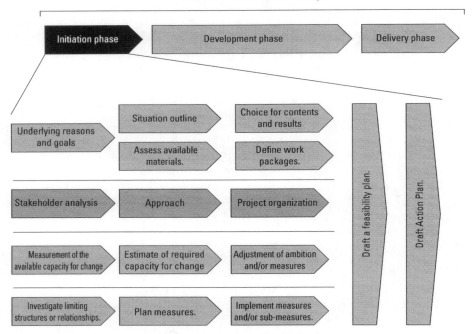

Figure 4.4   Activities at the level of 'willingness to change' in the initiation phase

dependent on the organization's situation. Key choices include the following (Stoop & Silvius, 2012):

1. Sponsorship - who is and feels responsible for the project? What management team members are the executives for the project? Executives have a great deal of influence if they actually support the project and demonstrate its value to others in an active and visible manner.
2. Staffing - which employees are participating in the project? A team with a mandate and the right knowledge is essential, preferably with members from different business disciplines and hierarchical levels.
3. The role of the IT department - what is the role of the IT department in the project? It may be counterproductive for IT to play too dominant a role, but inadequate involvement may result in the wrong choices for data and information systems.

4.1.3   Determine what is needed in order to balance ambition with capacity for change

To prevent a situation where it transpires there is not enough time, money or adequate quality capacity available to execute the project during the prioritization or execution of the business transformation plan, any issues or concerns should be brought to the attention of senior management at an early stage. Of course, definitive information on the required capacity for change will only be available at the end of the business transformation planning project. If, at that point, it turns out there is not enough capacity for change available, then the business transformation plan will provide nothing more than a set of projects that could have been implemented if the organization had the means to do so. That is why it is critical to get an idea of the capacity for change available in the organization at the earliest possible stage.

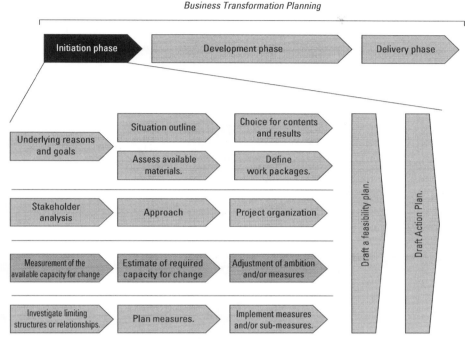

Figure 4.5   Activities at the level of capacity for change in the initiation phase

1. *Measurement of the available capacity for change*

First, it is important to obtain an insight into the features of the organization that are relevant to change management. Establishing whether major changes have been successfully implemented in the past and the degree to which people at different levels were willing and able to contribute says a great deal about an organization's change management qualities. In addition, it is useful to establish the organization's capacity to translate goals into actions and to work in a project-oriented way.

Yet capacity for change also includes 'harder' aspects, such as the number of internal hours available annually for improvement projects, what budget is available for changes and the organization's competencies in the area of change. Insight into these aspects is also crucial for making a proper estimate of the available capacity for change. Assessing the capacity for change in the initiation phase (on hard and soft aspects), rather than later on, gives us a useful picture at an early stage of the change that an organization can accomplish within a specific timeframe.

2. *Estimate of required capacity for change.*
As explained above, in the initiation phase we define the goals for the business transformation plan, prepare a situation outline and put together an inventory of the available resources. This can be helpful in establishing, at an early stage, the level of ambition and the capacity for change that are needed to implement the transformation.

3. *Adjust the ambition or take measures to increase the capacity for change.*
How do we proceed if the assessment indicates that the available capacity for change (in terms of time, money or quality) is less than that required for the transformation? In such a case the organization has two options to make its plans feasible:
• Attempt to increase its capacity for change;
• Adjust its ambitions for the business transformation (make them more realistic).

The intention is not so much to temper the ambitions, because a prioritization is always conducted to ensure that, where possible, the most critical tasks are completed first. It is in fact vital that we do not lose sight of reality. The goal is to draft a somewhat ambitious but definitely realistic business transformation portfolio, where project lead times take account of the organization's capacity for change.

Ensuring that ambitions are realistic and then expanding capacity for change in a timely manner will only increase the chances of success for the business transformation portfolio. This makes it easier (and more pleasant) to manage implementation of the change because the defined goals are actually attainable, increasing your chances of success.

4.1.4 Establish feasibility and applicability and develop an action plan for the next step

The initiation phase is essential because it identifies the applicability and feasibility of the business transformation plan. Establishing this is a key success factor in every business transformation planning project. In this process, we mainly examine the potential risks. What should we take into account in the project? What are the reasons for developing the business transformation plan and are there any particular reasons why we should not do so? This allows for full consideration of the different factors in order to determine the feasibility of the business transformation planning project in each situation.

One key objective of the initiation phase is for the executive, the authors of the plan and other stakeholders and parties involved in the environment to reach an agreement on the project. The initiation phase defines the goal of the planning, the questions that the project will answer and the scope. Based on this, we draft an approach and a plan for the activities to be performed. Finally, we make preparations to start the business transformation planning project. Thus, this initiation or 'reconnaissance' phase provides insight not only into its applicability, but also its feasibility.

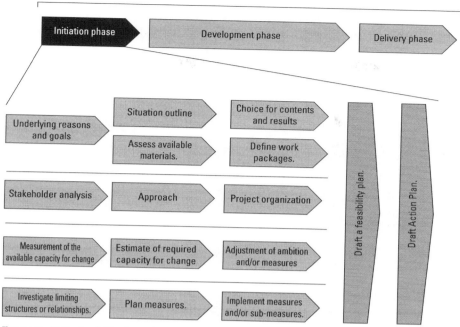

Figure 4.6   Draft a feasibility plan and action plan.

The aforementioned choices are then developed into a project proposal and submitted to the executive or steering committee for a decision. An agreement on this project proposal marks the conclusion of the initiation phase.

4.2   In the development phase, the plan is actually drawn up

The initiation phase is followed by the development phase. In this phase, the BTF is used to provide details of the business transformation plan for the various stakeholders. The action plan drafted in the initiation phase provides guidance on the activities to be performed in the development phase and their order of execution. Naturally, the result of this phase is a business transformation portfolio: a set of business transformation projects plotted over time, for which senior management define the prioritization. Chapters 2 and 3 covered the content of the execution phase in detail. However, the development phase also performs more activities and achieves more results at all four levels. Figure 4.7 shows the activities for the development phase. It clearly shows that developing a business transformation plan is a highly iterative process. The black lines and double arrows indicate that all activities can actually occur in any order, with the same activity often performed multiple times. The activities in the top row (in blue) are indeed in a logical order, but there is no real beginning or end.

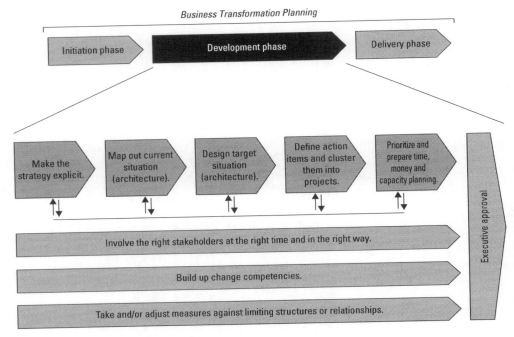

Figure 4.7   Activities in the development phase

4.2.1   Work in steps towards a specific and complete plan

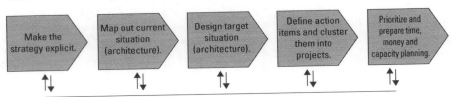

Figure 4.8   Activities in the development phase at the 'design' level

The activities needed to make the business transformation plan a reality are shown in figure 4.8 and correspond to the steps described in chapters 2 and 3. Although these chapters covered the BTF from the top down and from left to right, that is not typically how the plan is developed in practice. It is in fact iterative, without a clear starting point. In working out the plan, we also make ample use of visualizations and provide quantitative justification wherever possible.

1. *Work iteratively.*
It is practically impossible to go through the BTF all at once from top to bottom and left to right and end up with a complete, consistent and high quality business transformation plan. The design choices to be made might require new guiding principles. Constraints in the application landscape might reveal opportunities for improvement in processes and services, and drafting the business management portfolio might uncover gaps. Developing a plan using the BTF is by necessity an iterative process.

However, there are, in fact, choices to make in each iteration. One commonly used pattern is to explicitly define a strategy for proceeding through the columns from left to right in an initial iteration in order to gain insight and a holistic overview. This holistic overview will clarify the points where further details are needed in subsequent iterations, which can then be planned in a highly targeted manner.

Another way to approach an initial iteration is with themes. Themes are topics of concern to the organization at that time. These are often current case files, points for attention or ambitions of the board or the management. One major point to bear in mind when using themes is to ensure regular alignment and integration, so that we ultimately produce a single business transformation plan.

2. Use the power of visualization in a variety of ways.
Visual communication is a central feature of a business transformation plan, both in the project when creating the plan and in the final tangible results. The main reason for this is that in most cases 'a picture is worth a thousand words'. The final business transformation plan and its interim results will be better understood if good visualizations are used to explain the choices made, instead of, say, a 50-page report.

Therefore, visualizations make it easier to communicate the interim and end results of the business transformation plan. A single well constructed image can provide insight into complex materials, such as an organization's product catalog, which would normally require a great deal of text to explain. Incidentally, this does not mean that it reduces or simplifies the work. Because of the problem of omitting key points, it often takes more time to create a transparent and self-explanatory visualization than to write down what the image should convey. The benefits will not come until later, in the communication of the results. Each image has its own explanation to prevent misunderstandings and misinterpretations. Thus, the tangible results of a business transformation planning project often consist of three products:
1. The business transformation plan (rich in visualization);
2. A management presentation (summary);
3. A text summary or management memo.

3. Wherever possible, support all of the choices made with quantitative information.
The 'gut feeling' of a group of people sometimes works very well as a consensus model, but testing and supporting this feeling with the required quantitative data nevertheless often results in somewhat different, or even radically different, understandings and choices. Quantitative information is concerned with numbers and size, performances, costs and revenues, profitability or objectives.

One common pitfall when applying the framework for business transformation planning is trying to achieve alignment without taking any limitations that may exist into account. We see this kind of situation, for instance, when a particular application exhibits technical defects and frequent failures, creating delays in processes or interruptions in online services.

Without an awareness of factors such as volumes (how many units of a product are actually sold) and objectives, it is highly tempting to define an action item to address the problem. However, actually mapping out the quantitative information can reveal that the product in question is selling poorly and that the objective should be to phase the product out in two years.

4.2.2 Involve the right stakeholders at the right time and in the right way

Involve the right stakeholders at the right time and in the right way.

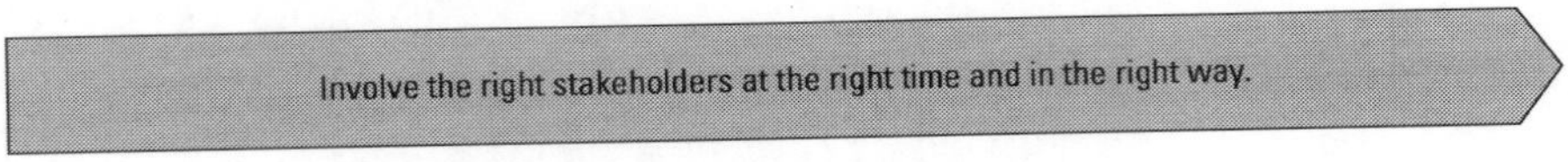

Figure 4.9   Activities in the development phase at the 'willingness' level

1. *Choose methods that maximize group performance.*
Arriving at an effective plan in terms of content takes more than just the involvement of the right people. The methods used are also crucial in order to achieve a well-structured and cohesive result within the agreed timeframe and ensure that this can be communicated successfully within the organization.

The BTF makes ample use of interactive methods to conduct analyses, prepare designs and make choices in combination. Different workshops – usually with multidisciplinary groups – brainstorm and discuss a predefined topic in a dynamic manner. One key guiding principle in this process is shared responsibility for delivering results.

Workshops are an effective and efficient way to achieve results in terms of content from a change management perspective. It is essential to the success of the workshop that all stakeholders have thoroughly prepared themselves. Depending on the participants, the topic for discussion and the purpose of the workshop, we determine the methods that will be used during the workshop. For instance, it may be very effective to hold a brainstorming session for a group of people who are highly risk-averse by nature in order to stimulate new ideas for solutions or opportunities. On the other hand, when working with a highly creative group, it may be wise to choose a method that helps all ideas converge in the same direction. If the goal of a workshop is validation, then different methods will be used than for a workshop that needs to set priorities or make choices.

In order for a workshop to succeed, it is important that the process is facilitated by a moderator who has not played a part in any of the discussions relating to content. This process moderator must continuously monitor the progress in achieving the goals, define frameworks for this and intervene when discussions are not moving forward or when conflicts or points of uncertainty arise. The moderator may also take on a role of 'challenging' or testing the group's opinions or choices to ensure they are well thought-out.

The matters decided upon during the workshop (guiding principles, choices, agreements etc.) should be documented, preferably by writing down the results as they happen during the workshop in a place visible to everyone. The final part of the workshop must always be reserved for a brief recap, including the identification of action items and allocation of tasks. It is important to provide feedback on workshop results, not only to validate the results, but also so that participants know their input was used and their contribution was worthwhile.

2. *Involve the right stakeholders at the right time and in the right way.*

In addition to the frequent use of workshops, employing a variety of methods, the principle of shared responsibility is also a key component of the collaboration process during planning. Participants in the core team share responsibility for delivery of the sub-products. They work out sub-results defined independently or in a group and present these to the rest of the core team. They also present workshops in their own area of expertise (possibly with facilitation, where needed) and involve others from the organization to provide input.

To ensure appropriate levels of support for the eventual business transformation plan, it is crucial to involve the right stakeholders in the process in a timely and proper manner. Roughly speaking, we have four types of stakeholders in a business transformation planning project:
1. Decision-makers (owners): directors/the management team.
2. Executive and any deputy executive.
3. Direct stakeholders: people directly involved in drafting the plan.
4. Indirect stakeholders: 'second circle' stakeholders who will be affected by the plan, or with whom a dependency exists.

Which stakeholders are involved is highly dependent upon the current phase of the business transformation plan. The execution phase, however, normally starts with elaborating the strategic framework. This provides direction in preparing the different columns. It is mainly the executive and the decision-makers who need to be involved at this level (the management level). They provide strategic direction to the organization (or business unit) and create a picture of where the organization wants to go.

When working out the objectives and pictures (vision) in detail in relation to the aspects of Customers & Services, Processes & Organization, Information & Applications and IT Infrastructure & Facilities, it is vital to involve people with specialist knowledge, in particular those who are recognized for this knowledge within the organization. The role they play will primarily focus on content. As soon as critical choices need to be made regarding the directions to take, it will be the decision-makers involved in the strategic framework who will play a crucial role.

During the process of working out the architectures, it is vital to involve a broad group of stakeholders, with the choice depending on the topic at hand. Some methods at your disposal here include directly involving experts, internal or external clients, a focus group or individual feedback. Once the candidate projects have been created, it is up to the decision-makers to approve them and set the associated priorities. They are ultimately the ones who determine the importance of the projects and the pace of change.

3. *The importance of effective communication.*
Good communication not only helps during business transformation planning, it is also crucial in subsequent phases. The project is, after all, step one of the change and change usually has a major impact on the people within organizations. A lack of information or the opportunity to ask questions and express concerns may result in resistance.

The target groups for communication follow on from the stakeholder analysis. Different target groups will have different information needs, and some information is less suitable for certain target groups. Creating a holistic overview – at the start of the business transformation planning – of the information to be communicated to the different target groups (an information matrix) enables us to establish clear agreements on this.

The method of communication often depends on the target group. Typically, we adopt the approach and structure that is already familiar to the organization. Here, 'method of communication' refers to the medium used, such as email, newsletters, intranet, reports/ notes, meetings, the opportunity to speak freely during discussions, personal contact, etc. We use a target group media matrix to define the method(s) of communication used for each target group.

The different forms and points of contact for communication must be aligned with the goal and the phase of business transformation planning. It is difficult to provide guidelines for this, but in practice we have identified a number of key communication moments during business transformation planning:
- Communication with the executive: this should take place throughout the entire project, guarantee involvement, stay on track and discuss any options or choices in a timely manner. Regular coordination with management ensures that the decision-making process does not result in any surprises.
- Kickoff: communication action plan for direct stakeholders and decision-makers. Collectively affirm and create the feeling that 'this is what we are going to do and the business transformation plan is the answer'. It is also a vital tool for expectation management: what do we expect of each other during this project?
- Communication about the architectures: in the business transformation plan, the architectures are content-heavy outlines that show what services, processes, etc., will look like in the future. These visualizations must come to life in the organization. Good communication regarding these architectures helps make them understandable for those stakeholders not involved in creating them.
- Communication of the final business transformation plan: from decision-makers (management) to the organization. Show that there is already a broad group of people behind it, how it came about, which 'experts' have been involved, how management supports the plan, what it will deliver and last but not least, that the plan is feasible.

When communicating the plan and the changes it will deliver, it is important to have clear agreements in place. These agreements must address the following:
- Adjustment of informal communication;
- Reducing the general levels of rumor and gossip surrounding the content of the plan;
- Promoting the right interpretation;
- Promoting dialog.

Finally, we have some practical tips related to communication during business transformation planning:
- Stick to your agreements. People often say they will produce and circulate information after workshops, but there is a risk that it will not actually happen. It is critical for stakeholders to recognize themselves in the business transformation plan and get the opportunity to add to it.
- In order to present and deliver your business transformation plan, it is preferable to use PowerPoint sheets (or Prezi, etc.) instead of a text document. This forces you to focus upon the key information and omit excessive detail. Always make the message central and use the framework as the backbone for the entire project.
- Validation is crucial because business transformation planning is carried out relatively quickly within a specific timeframe. Have the plan validated by a broader group, such as through a focus group. This works well in practice. In any case, it is important:
  - Not to present interim results as if they are set in stone, but rather to create opportunities for questions and concerns;
  - To bring participants into the process along with the considerations raised in order to arrive at the results;
  - Not to simply present the results, instead have the group 'live' the results themselves by talking them over.

4. *Apply some pressure by limiting the lead time.*
The lead time of business transformation planning is a key success factor. The lead time is usually limited to a maximum of four months, and is frequently less than that. In this timeframe, it must be possible to deliver a quality plan, with broad support, at the right level of abstraction. Business transformation planning is, therefore, conducted within a time box: aspects that need to be worked out in further detail in order to make certain choices will appear in the change management portfolio as a research proposal.

A limited lead time is essential in order to hold the organization's attention long enough to prevent the plan from becoming obsolete after it is developed. Incidentally, this does not mean that the timing of business transformation planning is rigid. It is possible to make certain urgent decisions during the project and start implementing them. Some examples here would be getting started on an organization plan or the improvement of the current management reports.

5. *Make sure the different teams have the right make-up.*
Ensuring the involvement of the right people during business transformation planning and eliciting their optimal guidance in order to maximize their impact will, in turn, maximize the likelihood of the organization making the right choices in order to attain its objectives.

On the one hand, on the project will benefit from the quality and diversity of the people involved. Business transformation planning requires different kinds of knowledge, experience and competencies. Bringing the right people into the team (core team, work streams, steering committee, focus group) minimizes the risk of oversights and ensures that the implications of the chosen direction are identified for all sub-areas.

On the other hand, the people involved must receive appropriate guidance in order to arrive at effective results. Essentially, this means providing incentives and facilitation for collaborating in the achievement of a properly structured, cohesive and communicable result that is delivered within the agreed timeframe.

In order to use a business transformation plan to achieve an organization's objectives, the final thing we still need to address is proper delivery to the line organization. This is the topic of the next section.

6. *Ensure a sound project organization and involve the right people in it.*
During the planning process, we must steer the project based on the quality of the plan in order to increase the chances of reaching our ambitions.

As mentioned previously, conducting a proper initiation phase at the start of the planning process, ensuring support for the plan and building up the organization's capacity for change are all essential to the project's success. However, if the content of the final plan is not of adequate quality, then the organization will still be unable to implement a successful change. This is why, during the planning process, we must steer the project in a way that focuses upon the quality of the plan's content. So, how do we ensure that the contents of the plan are of adequate quality? On the one hand, we can do this by involving the right people in the process and on the other hand, by shaping and executing the process in a way that gets the most out of everyone involved.

7. *Business transformation planning requires three kinds of competencies.*
First, we need people that bring *subject-matter expertise* to the table. This may be, for example, a marketing expert who knows the best way to attract new customers or an IT manager who understands how to interface different systems. In addition to this, we also need *organization-specific* knowledge of the organization itself, its customers and the market. Some examples here would be a production manager who can explain how the products that the organization supplies are manufactured, or a sales manager who knows the size of the market and the most profitable customer segments. Finally, we need *organizational* competencies, such as a process specialist who knows everything about process design or an

organization adviser who can provide consultation on the business transformation strategy to be used.

8. *Different working groups investigate specific topics.*
In addition to the core team, there are often one or more other work streams required during business transformation planning. A work stream investigates a particular issue or sub-issue, for which the core team lacks the capacity or knowledge, in detail. This is often a deeper analysis within a column of the BTF or at the interface level between two columns, which requires more subject matter and/or organization-specific knowledge than the core team has. The employees in the work stream carry out duties according to the task assigned, but they are primarily subject-matter experts. The 'president' of the work stream is a member of the core team and reports on the results and progress of the work stream.

9. *The steering committee is responsible for the project, for interim adjustment and for decision-making.*
In business transformation planning there is a need to implement a steering committee. Senior management are always represented on the steering committee. Steering committee tasks include drafting assignments, forming opinions and making decisions on content-related topics and evaluating the various interim and end results. The steering committee must also ensure there are adequate human and other resources to carry out the business transformation planning activities.

Aside from the core team, the work streams and the steering committee, we can also opt to use focus groups. This is optional, and sometimes the steering group performs this role. The focus group validates the interim results from the business transformation planning and indicates the degree of satisfaction of the rank and file of the organization. The purpose of the focus group is often to create a base of support in the relevant departments.

10. *The core team is responsible for the actual implementation of the plan.*
Involving the right people starts back in the initiation phase: in this phase, the main stakeholders are identified and what we call a 'core team' is formed. The scope of the business transformation plan (such as one particular department/business unit or the entire organization) is one factor that determines who is in the core team. This team goes through, lives through and controls the business transformation planning process and makes the 'final edit' to the definitive plan. The core team usually has the following roles (though multiple roles may actually be performed by the same person):
• Project manager (of business transformation planning);
• Business consultant and/or analyst;
• IT consultant and/or analyst;
• Various subject-matter experts (marketing, production, IT and other departments).

4.2.3　Use the lead time for planning to build up capacity for change

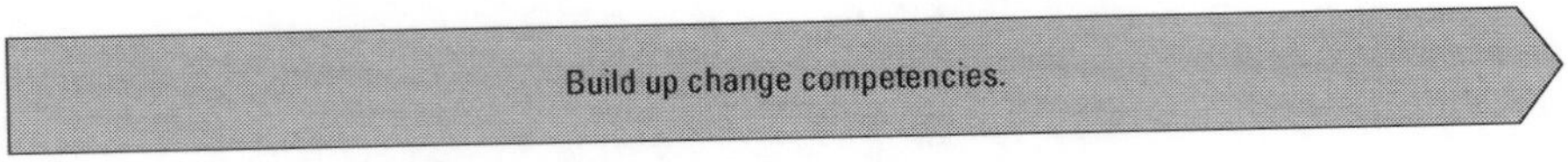

Figure 4.10　Activities in the development phase at the 'ability' level

Business transformation planning creates energy in advance of the change that is to come. In order to maintain that energy and use that momentum for the change, it is vital to make timely preparations for the execution of the business transformation portfolio. If the capacity for change does not appear to be adequate, it is a good idea to start expanding it during the project.

You must have practical resources available like time and money, but 'soft' capacity for change is at least as important. Aside from having enough people who are *willing* to change (see also section 4.2), this also means having people who are *able* to change. In order to lead and steer the change, these 'changers' must have the skills needed to implement the business transformation. Changers can be found at various levels and in various disciplines: directors, department heads, project managers, process/quality managers and IT managers. All of these people play an active role in implementing change and must therefore have the skills to lead, govern, inspire, motivate and move people to change.

Aside from the people leading and managing the change, employees in the organization are also stakeholders. Because new products must be brought to market, new procedures adopted or new information systems implemented, the people who perform this work must also change. In order to anticipate the upcoming changes, we should pay attention to including and developing people during the business transformation planning. One approach is individual training or coaching to acquire the knowledge and skills needed for a successful change.

A number of items are critical to ensuring that practical capacity for change (e.g. time and money) is available at the end of the business transformation planning. Firstly, the current projects that the organization is already carrying out, or are in the planning stage, should be included when prioritizing projects. This ensures that the change projects arising out of the business transformation plan are not added 'on top of' those projects already underway or planned in the organization, but rather that senior management should examine the big picture of the entire portfolio of projects and prioritize accordingly. This may mean stopping a project that was planned but is now considered less important in order to free up capacity to carry out a newly drafted change project from the business transformation plan.

Secondly, it is crucial to incorporate the results of the business transformation planning into the regular planning and control cycle of the organization. If an organization delivers its annual plan for the upcoming year for approval in September, for example, it would not make much sense to record the results of the business transformation planning and a corresponding capacity and budget claim in November. It would certainly not make sense for an organization that is to be tightly controlled and evaluated based on the implementation of the annual plan. Therefore, the business management portfolio must be adjusted appropriately before the annual plans are finalized, so that the necessary resources are taken into account within the annual plan. This prevents ending up with an annual plan that fails to factor in the time and money for execution of the business transformation plan. It also reduces the risk of an inability to carry out these change projects.

Thirdly, senior management must be committed to making additional time and money available, where needed, in order to execute the business transformation plan. Despite the fact that the specific time and budget requirements will only become visible at the end of the business transformation planning exercise, there is in fact always a concern as to whether the organization will have enough resources to execute the business transformation plan in the near future. If it appears that there may be problems then measures can be taken at an early stage, such as bringing in or hiring one or more project managers or outsourcing regular work so that internal staff can concentrate on the execution of the business transformation plan.

4.2.4 The executive must take ownership of, and approve the plan

Figure 4.11   Activities in the development phase: approval of the plan by the executive.

The result of the development phase is the actual business transformation plan. If additional work is nevertheless required in the delivery phase before discharging the project team, it is critical for the executive to officially approve the plan during this stage. This is because all activities in the delivery phase are geared towards the proactive and rapid execution of the planned change.

4.3   The delivery phase ensures that the organizational change can start right away

Business transformation planning is usually carried out via a number of smaller projects. This means that the project organization set up to deliver the business transformation plan will be disbanded. However, the plan still needs to be carried out and however good your planning may be, multi-year plans are never set in stone. The plan must, therefore, be maintained and the responsibility for this must 'land' somewhere. Back in the planning stage, we ensured that all of the results and sub-results of the plan could be allocated to different departments, teams and employees, and that the processes for maintaining and updating the business transformation plan could be implemented. Figure 4.12 shows the activities carried out in the delivery phase.

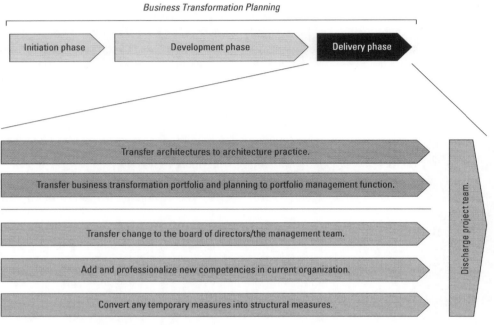

Figure 4.12   Activities in the delivery phase

We have already covered why it is essential to involve the right people during the planning process and properly support them in arriving at a feasible and high quality business management plan. Therefore, delivery of the business transformation plan and other results to the current organization (line organization) is something that would logically happen at the end of the business transformation planning.

However, delivery is actually an activity that takes place continuously over the process with the right people at the right time, working together in the right way. So, what needs to happen in order to ensure that the business transformation plan is well received in the line organization? We will discuss this in the subsections below.

4.3.1   The architecture role uses the guiding principles and architectures and further develops them

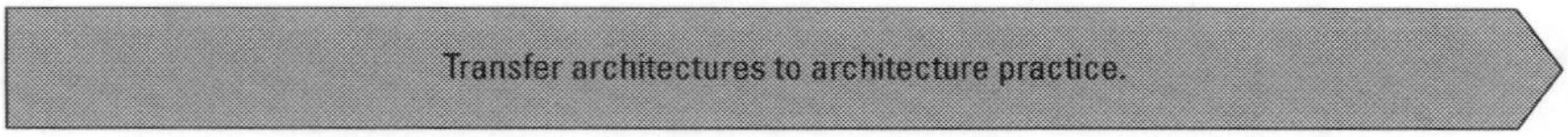

Transfer architectures to architecture practice.

Figure 4.13   Activities in the delivery phase at the 'design' level

Chapter 2 goes into detail about the guiding principles and architectures developed in the planning process. These guiding principles and architectures must be delivered to the architecture function in the organization. In fact, this delivery will actually have already occurred by bringing in architects during the business transformation planning. At the end of the planning process, only the formal delivery remains.

In the development phase of the business transformation plan, we draft the guiding principles and architectures in conjunction with the architects available. It is certainly not always necessary for these architects to be people with the job title 'architect' on their business card. For instance, it may be a marketing director or a product manager who goes over the product catalog (making this person the architect for part of the first column) and a quality manager who is responsible for a consistent internal process model. In other words, it can be people in the organization who perform the <u>role</u> of architect (for their area), but whose <u>job title</u> is not architect.

The initiation phase quickly makes it clear whether (formal or informal) architects are available in the organization, and if so, who they are. This is because this phase includes requesting all manner of documentation on areas such as current products and services, how processes are designed and the available applications. If this architecture role is lacking in one or more area within an organization, then attention must be given to its creation during the business transformation planning. The aim here is to enable proper allocation of the content results after completion of the business transformation plan and adjustments based on this during the change.

4.3.2   All programs, projects and plans are implemented by the portfolio management role

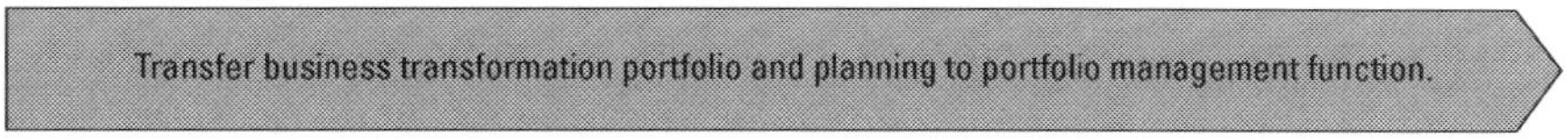

Transfer business transformation portfolio and planning to portfolio management function.

Figure 4.14   Activities in the delivery phase at the 'design' level

In addition to activities of the line organization, the business transformation plan also contains two kinds of projects: (1) precondition projects and (2) priority projects.

These projects can be either candidate or actual projects arising out of the business transformation plan and may be preplanned or ongoing projects. During the business transformation planning, all projects are then included in a draft project charter, which describes the key features of each project. Next, management assigns priorities to the projects. Once the projects have been prioritized, the business transformation portfolio is created. For this, a schedule is created along with a capacity plan and budget, taking into account priorities and interdependencies. Ideally the project prioritization and planning activities should be developed in close collaboration with Portfolio Management or Project Portfolio Management (PPM). At the end of the business transformation planning, the business transformation portfolio is formally delivered to the PPM role.

We do not wait until the end of the business transformation planning to approach the PPM role: this person should be involved from the beginning. This is because the PPM also plays a key role in putting together an inventory of ongoing projects and project initiatives during the initiation phase, at the same time as when a picture of the organization's capacity for change is established. Later in the project, the PPM role is also heavily involved in estimating the number of projects that can be carried out simultaneously over a particular period of time without exceeding the organization's capacity for change. Consequently, it is already clear at the initiation phase whether the PPM function or role is present in the organization. At that point, there is still enough time left to set this role up during the planning process, or at least a basic version of it, if necessary. This is important in order to prevent the projects from the business transformation portfolio from experiencing difficulty landing in the line organization after completion of the business transformation planning.

4.3.3   Identified change activities in the line organization are allocated in the regular planning cycle

As stated in section 2.5, when drafting the business transformation portfolio, a subdivision is created consisting of actions to be allocated to the line organization along with projects to be prioritized. Activities allocated to the line organization have the following characteristics:
* They belong to the primary task of a department;
* Interaction with other departments is generally unnecessary;
* No separate control from management is needed;
* Additional resources are not needed.

Therefore, no projects are initiated for these activities. Instead, we determine the department to which each activity belongs together with the manager who is responsible for performing the activity. The activities to be undertaken in a department are discussed with the responsible departmental manager. These activities are controlled using the regular planning & control cycle for running the organization. In cases of any dependencies with programs and projects in the business transformation portfolio, the performance of the activities in the line organization is monitored from the business transformation portfolio. After all, nothing should be left to chance, if possible.

4.3.4   The board and the management take responsibility for implementation of the change

Transfer change to the board of directors/the management team.

Figure 4.15   Activities in the delivery phase at the 'will' level

Implementing organizational change is, in fact, always a direct responsibility of the board of directors or senior management. Thus, they have ownership of the change, or they must acquire it. Separately from the formal acceptance of the business transformation plan, aside from granting the project team their discharge, it is far more important here for the board of directors or management to take ownership and responsibility for the change described in the business transformation plan, in a visible manner that is clear to the entire organization.

The board/management has various options for showing that they are taking on ownership and responsibility of the change. One way is to hold open, interactive sessions. These have the most impact. Often, the board goes on a 'roadshow' to the different departments. Another option is a plenary kickoff. Modern variants include live chats and webcasts.

4.3.5 New competencies are stored in the permanent organization and further professionalized

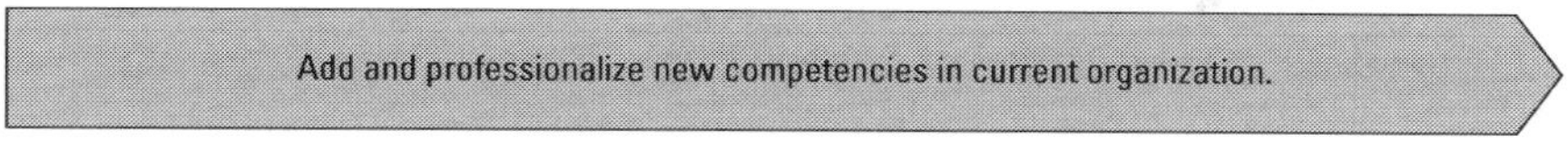

Add and professionalize new competencies in current organization.

Figure 4.16   Activities in the delivery phase at the 'ability' level

The delivery of guiding principles and architectures, activities to the line organization and projects to the relevant roles/departments is vital in order for a business transformation plan to land properly in the line organization. Depending on whether or not the overall project is guided by an external party, there may be one more action: delivery of the methodology-specific knowledge related to the BTF itself. Whether this knowledge needs to be transferred depends on whether the organization wishes to be able to implement the BTF itself in the future without external support. Smaller organizations will not typically perform enough of these projects (e.g. for each business unit or process chain) to invest in the development of internal knowledge. For larger organizations, however, it may be useful to have in-house staff on hand who can effectively support these kinds of projects. Through appropriate training and coaching, in-house staff can be taught to use the BTF on their own.

4.3.6 The project team responsible for drafting the business transformation plan is granted formal discharge

Developing a business transformation plan according to the BTF is a project in itself. It requires resources to be freed up and tight guidance towards achieving several clear results, not least of which is the business transformation plan itself. In this kind of approach, it is also appropriate for the executive to grant discharge to the project leader and the project team upon completion of the plan. In terms of projects, whilst this is an important time, as stated earlier, it is also highly symbolic. Once the business transformation planning project team is discharged, it is up to the organization itself to implement the change.

4.4   Summary

In this chapter, we showed that the process of business transformation planning is more than just writing a business transformation plan. During business transformation planning, we perform activities at four levels:
1. Design – the content of the plan.
2. Willingness – the readiness for change.
3. Ability – the capacity for change.
4. Conditioning – removing obstacles to change.

Drafting the business transformation plan itself is about clarifying the strategy, gaining insight into and analyzing the current situation, designing the target situation and deriving and planning the required change activities. The framework for business transformation planning described in chapters 2 and 3 plays the main role in this process.

During planning, we deploy several activities with the aim of ensuring that the organization will carry out the plan. For this, large groups of stakeholders must lend their support to the proposed change. Generally, this will only happen if they themselves were able to influence the plan, either directly or indirectly through colleagues.

Of course, in addition to this, we also examine whether the organization is actually able to implement the change. This depends upon the required resources and competencies. At an early stage, we determine whether the level of ambition is in line with the organization's capacity for change. If it is not, then we can use the lead time for the planning to expand the capacity for change. Another option is to adjust our ambitions downwards.

Finally, we take an explicit look at the obstacles to change. This typically includes counterproductive aspects of the organization's culture, relationship patterns or structures. These are often the reasons why changes were unsuccessful in the past. It is critical to take measures to remove or neutralize these obstacles.

Business transformation planning features three phases:
1. An initiation phase in which the goal is optimal preparation for the subsequent phases.
2. The development phase, in which the business transformation plan is actually made.
3. Finally, the delivery phase, which ensures that all components of the business transformation plan 'land' in the permanent organization so the change is implemented according to plan.

5 A good business transformation plan is the single best management tool for implementing a business transformation portfolio

The number of business transformation plans made is far greater than the number of ongoing or completed organizational changes. This is simply because many business transformation plans end up getting filed away, stall during execution or are canceled due to lack of feasibility. Obviously this is not on purpose. That is why we do everything we can during the planning phase to avoid such outcomes. First, we make certain that we have a solid, well thought-out, realistic and broadly supported business transformation plan. (Section 4.3 describes the engineering of the business transformation plan.) In addition to this, during the planning phase, we must also pay attention to the organization's capacity for change and, where necessary and possible, apply or initiate improvements. Despite our best preparations, however, setting the business transformation in motion will still be fairly tricky. This is not unusual. In practice, we have seen that this has a great deal to do with the switch from planning changes on paper to implementing changes in reality. Whereas the planning is still quite 'safe' in terms of costs, risks and potential consequences, this is certainly not the case when it comes to implementing the business transformation portfolio. Actual deployment of the organizational changes involves hefty investments, a great deal of risk, a necessary degree of uncertainty and, invariably, surprises as well. Naturally, this means that high-impact organizational changes require strong leadership and bold action by the board of directors and management. Moreover, it also requires specific competencies, which for many organizations are not familiar. However, in addition to leadership, we have also seen in practice that having a sound business transformation plan as a management tool – in combination with the right competencies – also considerably reduces initial resistance and increases the likelihood of success. In section 5.1, we will explain how an organization can use a business transformation plan for managing the business transformation and which competencies are required to maintain and execute the plan.

Another complication in managing the business transformation is the interdependency between 'running the organization' and 'changing the organization'. Naturally, an organization cannot simply close its doors for an extended period of time in order to implement an organizational change. Every day – organizational change or not – the organization must continue providing services to customers, patients or citizens. While it is usually possible to find the capacity for drafting a business transformation plan (although it is often on top of the regular activities of those involved), this is certainly not the case when it comes to implementing a business transformation portfolio. It requires a lot more money, management attention and staff capacity over a much longer period of time. Thus, the implementation of organizational changes is not isolated from day-to-day operations.

This means it is vital to coordinate the 'change' activities and the 'run' activities. Changing with the 'doors open' is the topic of section 5.2.

5.1 The business transformation plan is the master plan for all change activities

Chapters 1 to 4 explained how to elaborate an organization's ambitions using guiding principles and architectures and ultimately a business transformation portfolio consisting of programs, projects and change activities. The business transformation plan is, therefore, a key management tool for the management. Using a business transformation plan for managing the business transformation ensures that the organization stays focused on implementing its strategic ambitions and that resources are effectively allocated for this. But it is no magic wand. It takes a lot to effectively implement the business transformation plan. For this reason, organizations require specific competencies and specific governance mechanisms.

First, an organization – and more specifically the board of directors, the general management and the program and project management – must have the change management competencies needed to guide the employees involved in the change. However, organizational changes also have a structural component. Specifically, this means we must also design and implement product changes, new distribution channels, modernized processes, procedures and applications, etc. Figure 5.1 shows the competencies an organization needs to manage the structural component of organizational changes. This encompasses the entire process of realizing organizational changes.

The competencies in Figure 5.1 are highly interrelated and ideally will all be at the same level of maturity. It all starts with defining the organization's strategy, which, as mentioned above, is also the starting point of the BTF. The programs and projects that we have identified in the business transformation plan must be executed. This requires program and project management competencies. In the section on creating the business transformation plan, we covered working with architectures and thinking in terms of a business transformation portfolio. These are still two highly critical management practices for managing programs and projects. Management of the business transformation portfolio optimizes value creation and allocation of resources. Architecture management monitors the implementation of the transformation from a content perspective, thus ensuring structural and future-proof solutions. Within programs and projects, we need the competencies of implementation and business design in order to make the change a reality.

Therefore, in addition to project and program management for managing and executing individual projects and programs, business transformation portfolio management and architecture management are also key governance mechanisms. Therefore, we must further describe management of the business transformation portfolio and architecture management.

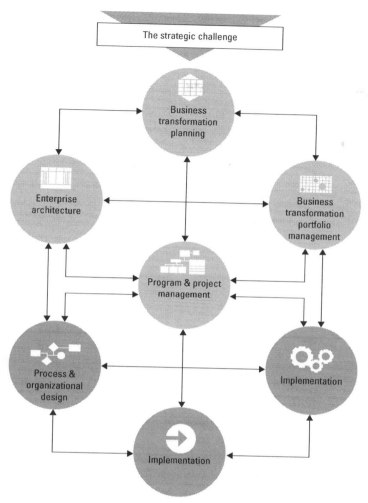

Figure 5.1 Novius Business Empowerment Framework: competencies needed for organizational change

In chapters 1 to 4, you have already learned what a business transformation plan is and how it is engineered. In this chapter, we will discuss updating, adjusting and, of course, using the business transformation plan for continuous management of the business transformation.

5.1.1 When managing the business transformation portfolio, the focus is on value creation and an optimal distribution of resources

A business transformation portfolio is drafted in the planning phase. As described in chapter 2, the business transformation portfolio includes the planning for programs, projects and business transformation activities, all of which are necessary, with their interrelationships, in order to achieve the planned changes. Project selection and planning are based on weighing the value created by the project against its risk of failure. The added-value of a project is derived directly from the contribution towards the organization's strategic goals or towards ensuring continuity. It is crucial to ensure a good balance between value and risk in the business transformation portfolio in order to optimize the added-value of the portfolio.

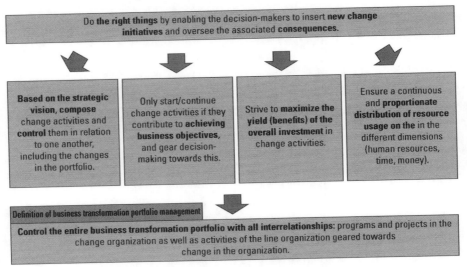

Figure 5.2 Definition and objectives of business transformation portfolio management

Once we have used the business transformation plan to put together a business transformation portfolio with an optimal mix of added-value and risk, it is vital to continuously adjust the business transformation portfolio in line with the latest insights. That is why we must design a management process within the organization for the business transformation portfolio. This business capability/competency ensures cohesion, as well as the monitoring and control of dependencies between the business transformation activities. It optimizes the use of available resources. This makes it possible to attain the results and benefits. After all, new programs, projects or activities may be proposed, projects may change in their objective or scope and they may be scrapped or go over schedule, budget or capacity. In addition to this, the appraisal of the added-value and the risks may change over time due to new insights or circumstances.

Thus, a business transformation portfolio includes multiple projects. Management of the business transformation portfolio is a continuous process focusing on the entirety of the projects in the portfolio *and* on the change activities assigned to the line organization so that, on the whole, the business transformation portfolio always features the optimal mix of added-value and risk. A business transformation portfolio may also include one or more programs and, naturally, the activities of the line organization. In section 2.5, we saw how the BTF process can allocate action items to the line organization. For this reason, we have found that monitoring these activities of the line organization and adjusting them as needed are also part of business transformation portfolio management. This is not the case in most methods for portfolio management (such as MoP® and PMI's Standard for Portfolio Management).

The process of managing the business transformation portfolio starts with the initial creation of the business transformation portfolio. Section 4.3 explained the engineering. From then on, the portfolio manager bears responsibility for the business transformation portfolio in the organization. The process of managing the business transformation portfolio features at least the following sub-processes:

- Maintaining the business transformation portfolio: adjust the business transformation portfolio in line with the latest information.
- Assess and provide advice on new or modified projects: determine the impact of proposals for projects or change on the business transformation portfolio (added-value and risk) so the Change Board or other committee can decide whether or not to include the project in the business transformation portfolio.
- Report on the portfolio: report on the status and progress of the projects in the portfolio, the change activities in the line organization and their impact on the overall business transformation portfolio.
- Resource planning: manage the available resources and capacity for change.
- Evaluate projects: determine whether the added-value of the project has been or will be achieved.

Figure 5.3 shows the interrelationships between these processes, business transformation planning and program and project execution.

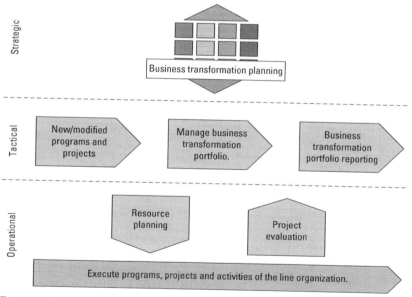

Figure 5.3   Processes in business transformation portfolio management

We will now further discuss the process of assessing and deciding on new or modified projects, the process of evaluating projects and the need for effective resource planning.

1. *The business transformation portfolio is not a static plan.*

The purpose of portfolio management is to identify the optimal balance between the value from the activities and the use of scarce resources, taking into account the risks and opportunities which may arise due to environmental factors as well as attainment of the organization's strategic objectives. Management of Portfolios (MoP®) is a framework that provides structured support for this. Organizational thinking is based on a strategy (ideally at least). In order to achieve the strategy, the organization must do something: it must go through a unique transformation. Limited resources are available for this. This is a balancing act between running an organization and changing the business. Portfolio management is the discipline that ensures the strategy is carried out in a controlled manner. MoP® provides a direct connection with the frameworks and methods for project and program management, such as PRINCE2®, MSP® and P3O® and M_o_R® for risk management. We have added a couple of points to this: see Figure 5.4.

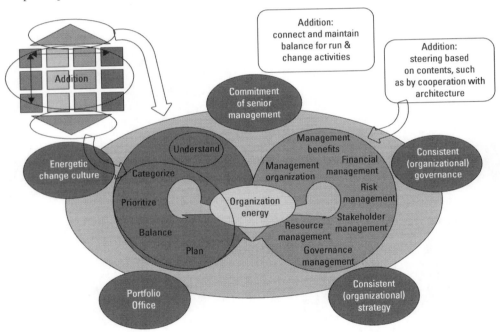

Figure 5.4   BTF management additions to the MoP® framework by AXELOS (based on source: AXELOS, 2011)

On the left side of the model, the BTF provides a detailed approach for clarifying the changes in order to achieve the strategic goals. On the right side of the model, the MoP® framework provides additional processes for managing the portfolio, which is the result of the BTF.

In our opinion, the right side of the MoP® framework doesn't cover the architecture management process to ensure the realization of future proof solutions. The target architecture developed in the business transformation plan (and possibly also worked out into an enterprise target architecture) serves as the guideline in the architecture management process (see also section 5.1.2.). Furthermore, we add managing changes that are assigned to the responsible management (instead of projects) as part of managing the business transformation portfolio. See Figure 5.5.

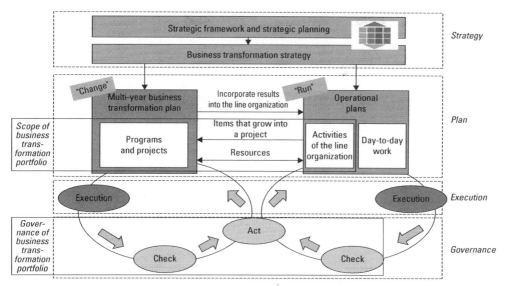

Figure 5.5   Distinction between steering for programs and projects versus activities of the line organization

In practice, many organizations set up a separate decision-making structure for portfolio management. In these decision-making structures, project owners discuss – at the management level – the prioritization, progress and results and benefits achieved for the projects and programs in the business transformation portfolio. This is really about the degree to which the organization is achieving its strategic goals by successful execution of projects in the portfolio. Management of activities of the line organization is also a key component here. Currently we see in practice that larger organizations often have a portfolio board set up, consisting of managers who advise the board of directors. In smaller organizations, the board of directors usually makes the portfolio decisions itself. The management of activities in the line organization is handled by the management team itself. Business transformation portfolio management has a holistic overview over the projects and programs as well as the activities of the line organization. The preparation of decision-making, advice and reporting of progress and issues is handled by the portfolio management process.

In our experience, it is best not to mix portfolio management with operational issues. It is preferable to handle business transformation portfolio management by means of a separate discussion (such as a separate management team session). If these topics are not separated, there is a high risk of spending too much time on operational and urgent matters and not getting around to making key decisions on the portfolio. In this way, an organization may 'push away' its strategic goals.

A medium-sized insurance organization used to manage projects separately. This resulted in a large number of steering committees (one per project) and burdened managers with participation in numerous steering committees. In addition, the board of directors lacked an overall view of all projects, and organization-wide projects were rarely taken on. To resolve these problems, a business transformation portfolio was worked out for the entire organization. This business transformation portfolio was prepared in conjunction with the management and approved by the board of directors. In order to implement the business transformation portfolio, a portfolio board was set up, with representatives appointed by management from all business units. One of the directors chaired the portfolio board, which met monthly. The portfolio manager prepared for the portfolio board by conducting analyses on the progress and status of the projects in the portfolio and by submitting proposals for new or modified projects for decisions. The portfolio board had the authority to make decisions as long as it did not exceed the budget granted by the board of directors.

2. *Project evaluation is necessary in order to keep the change under control.*
In order to manage the portfolio based on added-value, it is important to be able to determine and monitor project values. And this is precisely the hard part in practice, since many value estimates for projects are either qualitative in nature or not well supported. Methods such as Net Present Value (NPV) or Economic Value Added (EVA) are underutilized. These evaluation methods do require some data, which is often unavailable or difficult to track down. Nevertheless, it is still a good idea to make appropriate estimates of the project values. If adequate management information has not yet been collected to measure this properly, then start by taking small steps. Start with four to six strategic measurement values (KPIs) derived from the main CSFs. Then define the added-value for these four to six measurement points. In situations where a value estimate is not substantiated by arguments and figures, reality will undoubtedly turn out differently. In these cases, we cannot draw many conclusions from this difference, except perhaps that the estimate of the project's value was wrong. This is often a good opportunity to expand the number of KPIs or refine existing ones. However, project decisions must be based on more than just quantitative estimates.

It is also vital to continue measuring a project's added-value after its completion. Unfortunately, it rarely occurs in practice that organizations measure the benefits actually achieved after completion of a project. This is strange, because they normally pay a great deal of attention to drafting business cases that assume the value actually added by the project can only be enjoyed after delivery. It's as if afterwards, it is no longer important to determine whether the project achieved the business case. As a result, the organization is unable to learn how to construct better estimates for businesses cases for future projects. In practice, this is very important, and organizations do want this, but they lack good management information. So make certain, when starting small, that the KPIs you want to measure are in fact actually measurable.

Finally, good management and reporting will only meet with success with the right set of CSFs and KPIs. These must be monitored in annual planning reports. The same also applies to estimates of project costs. If we do not have the right CSFs and the KPIs derived from them, it will still be difficult to put together good estimates of project values and keep the transformation under control.

3. *In order to implement the business transformation plan, the funds and resources must be effectively allocated.*

Business transformation management is about more than just value creation. Project execution also requires the use of company resources. In addition to value optimization, the management of the business transformation portfolio should also be based on feasibility.

The feasibility of the business transformation portfolio is determined by the degree to which the organization's capacity for change is able to meet the cumulative resource needs of the projects in the business transformation portfolio. 'Resources' may include expertise, capacity (staff) and funds. As discussed in chapter 2, business transformation portfolios are often far too ambitious due to a failure to take the organization's capacity into account, or because of a lack of understanding regarding the resources the project requires. For this reason, during the BTF process, one should continuously examine the available and required capacity in order to produce a realistic business transformation portfolio.

However, even if a business transformation portfolio appears to be feasible, this feasibility may come under strain. For example, projects need more resources than originally planned, they need the planned resources for a longer period of time (because they are behind schedule), certain resources are no longer available (perhaps due to long-term illness) or resources may be withdrawn to resolve urgent issues in other new projects.

Careful monitoring and management of the availability and use of resources is a key component of business transformation portfolio management. This concerns the risk component of the business transformation portfolio. The progress of projects and the use of resources must be examined over the entire business transformation portfolio. Shuffling resources from one project to another may provide a quick fix in cases where a high-priority project is falling behind schedule, but this is not without consequences. The same applies if a project gets behind schedule. Because this project needs resources for a longer period of time, other projects that require the same resources will inevitably suffer delays. These considerations should be discussed in decision-making structures such as the portfolio board, where project owners oversee implementation of the business transformation portfolio. So, aside from value creation, the risks of the projects in the business transformation portfolio must also be managed in an integrated manner.

5.1.2   Architecture management ensures structured and future-proof business transformations

An organization can use business transformation portfolio management to ensure that projects that make optimal contributions towards strategic goals can be carried out in a planned and controlled manner. The planned target situation (also called the situation 'to-be' or the future state) implemented by the projects in the business transformation portfolio is described in the architectures for the business transformation plan. (See chapter 2.) Along with the guiding principles, these architectures serve as guidelines for the realization of the business transformation. Consequently, the organization steers itself based on the results and quality of the change.

Just like the business transformation portfolio, the architectures are static representations of the target situation, as defined at a given moment. In the meantime, the organization is exposed to all kind of changes, resulting from both internal and external factors. Market conditions change, constraints form, new needs arise and decisions have unintended consequences. The guiding principles and architectures taken from the business transformation plan are further detailed as part of the different projects, so each project contributes towards the implementation of the designed target situation. In practice, it is often the case that a design of the planned target situation is incomplete when a project is initiated. This means it is questionable whether the planned business transformation objectives will actually be achieved. Moreover, this often results in further discussions between stakeholders, leading to inevitable delays. To prevent this from happening, we must design an architecture management process. We use the phrase 'working under architecture' to describe those companies with an architecture management process that has been designed and actually implemented in practice.

Architecture management is a cyclical process that ensures:
- Advice and support for creating the strategy and business transformation planning process;
- Definition and maintenance of the enterprise target architecture;
- Definition of project architectures and advice for project execution;
- Advice for, and supervision of, the application of architecture frameworks.

We will not go into further detail on 'Advice and support for creating the strategy and business transformation planning process' by the architecture roles, because this has already been covered in chapter 2. However, we will explain the other three processes briefly below.

1. *The enterprise-specific architecture documents define and further maintain the guiding principles and architectures for the business transformation plan.*
The enterprise target architecture comprises the starting point for all projects that are carried out. New insights are progressively incorporated into this enterprise target architecture. This way, it is constantly being improved and elaborated. The enterprise target architecture is often written in a more formal language, such as ArchiMate, using special tools for architecture development and definition. This helps monitor for consistency and considerably increases maintainability. It also makes enterprise target architecture the most important deliverable in the architecture management process and project architectures are derived from it. Of

course, business transformation planning also uses the enterprise target architecture, if available. Furthermore, for some industries, there are industry-specific architectures available that can be used for designing the enterprise target architecture. For instance, banks and insurance companies make use of reference architectures.

2. *Using project architectures can accelerate working towards a solution that fits the organization's long-term vision.*

At the start of a project an expanded architecture of the intended target situation is developed, commonly known as a project start architecture (or PSA). A PSA turns the general architecture principles and models in the enterprise target architecture into an architecture tailored specifically to the project (Wagter et al. 2005). On the one hand, this limits the project's mandate for making decisions. On the other hand, it can accelerate work towards a solution that fits the organization's long-term vision. In combination with the project plan, the PSA is a management tool for the project. During project execution, a PSA provides direction for expanding the design for the project deliverables.

3. *Project deliverables and optimizations in operational management are tested to determine whether they meet the principles and architectures.*

Another objective of the architecture management process is to oversee compliance with the principles and architectures. We must determine whether the various project results meet the principles and architectures from the enterprise target architecture or the project Start Architecture. The same goes for all adjustments and optimizations in operational management that are considered to be outside of the project(s). In practice, this results in a variety of discussions, as it should. This is because we may encounter situations where new insights require an adjustment to the enterprise target architecture or the project start architecture, or where strong arguments arise for deviating from the enterprise target architecture. The latter may occur, for instance, if a product introduction needs to be rolled out before a specific time in order to be on the market first, which means 'some corners need to be cut'. In all cases, the choice should be a conscious decision made in consultation with the project owner, project manager and architect. The decisions made on this must be clearly documented. In the event of a conscious decision to deviate from the architecture, the consequences of this deviation must be clear. Preferably, we should also establish how we will still end up complying with the enterprise target architecture further down the road.

5.1.3   Program and project management ensures that things get done right

Planning has been completed, the design has been outlined and it is now time for implementation. Program and project management ensure that the associated activities are carried out correctly and efficiently. This also includes the change activities in the line organization that are typically handled as part of projects.

5.1.4   The BTF ensures the business transformation plan is updated and adjusted as necessary

A business transformation plan is not set in stone. In this modern era this is no longer desirable. It may be necessary to update or adjust the business transformation plan for a variety of reasons. However, it is important not to simply go along with every suggested update. There is often an overabundance of new ideas, proposals for improvement and opportunities. Consequently, the board of directors and management must always weigh these impulses against maintaining a predefined course. Without a steady course, an organization runs the risk of a large number of half-completed changes eating up the budget whilst failing to deliver the promised changes, and increasing the complexity of the organization.

Below we distinguish five reasons to update or adjust a business transformation plan by means of the BTF:

1. <u>New management</u>. When a new board of directors, a new director, manager or new management team takes over, a 'game plan' for the next two to four years is often needed. In many organizations, this corresponds to the average term of office for a manager. The new management often feels the urge to put their own ideas and ambitions in place, and these are likely to influence the strategy and therefore the planned target situation. There is not necessarily anything wrong with this, in fact it is often one of the reasons for shuffling management around. However, we should bear in mind the point made above about maintaining the course.

2. <u>New strategy</u>. When changing the strategy, we are obviously also changing course. This requires a complete review of the business transformation plan.

3. <u>High-impact changes</u>. Apart from the most urgent changes, it is especially vital to refrain from reacting too quickly and launching projects too fast. It is usually beneficial to take a little time to adjust the business transformation plan. In doing so, the proposed changes can be judged in conjunction with all other possible changes that the organization would like to realize. This can shed light on the likely impact of the changes and interdependencies, so that any possible synergies can be achieved. In many cases, the necessary adjustment can be completed in one or two weeks.

4. <u>Annual planning cycle</u>. We often see that the annual planning cycle is used as a trigger to start a BTF project. It may well be that the current business transformation plan is still up-to-date and the organization is on track in its implementation. In this case, we can update the plan rather quickly and at very low costs to the organization. This usually involves adjusting the architectures to the latest insights, updating the business transformation portfolio and holding a limited number of workshops to work out a few new topics or issues in enough detail to enable planning. In organizations that use what is known as a 'rolling forecast' (one planning cycle update every quarter), this also includes the architectures of the business transformation plan.

5. <u>Adjustments to the architecture</u>. The enterprise architecture also evolves over time. As projects are carried out, we make adjustments to the enterprise architecture as and when new information arises. These changes also need to be incorporated into the business transformation plan.

Thus, there are several different reasons to update or adjust a business transformation plan. This means the approach is never the same. That is why our message here is clear - always start with an initiation phase (see chapter 4). In this initiation phase, determine what needs to happen to update and adjust the business transformation plan properly, and identify which methods are suitable and how much time, money and capacity it will take.

5.2   The business transformation plan helps align day-to-day operations with process improvement and change

In some respects, star athletes and their support teams have it much easier than the vast majority of organizations. Naturally they must be at peak performance during a game, but before and afterwards they have plenty of time to train and improve their tactics, equipment and technique. However, most organizations must perform every day while also making improvements and being expected to prepare and implement organizational changes with some degree of regularity. This is not easy, and it demands a great deal of any organization.

We can distinguish between three types of operational processes in organizations:
1. They provide products and services that they use to serve their customers and run the processes needed for this. This is the day-to-day operation of an organization and is often referred to by the term RUN (for running an organization).
2. Organizations are constantly improving their products, services and processes in their day-to-day operations. We call this continuous improvement.
3. Structural organizational changes are regularly applied in all aspects of running a business.

Continuous improvement and organizational change are collectively referred to by the term CHANGE.

The three types of operational processes are of three different natures, with different dynamics, methods of control and required competencies. Table 5.1 shows the differences.

Therefore, we can distinguish between day-to-day operation, continuous improvement and organizational change because they are very different from one another. However, these three types of operations also feature dependencies. They are very closely interrelated, on three main points in particular:
1. Their common goal to achieve the same strategy and objectives.
2. They share the same resources: staff capacity, budget and management attention.
3. They exchange requirements, opportunities for improvement, structural changes and process improvements.

Figure 5.6 shows that day-to-day operation, continuous improvement and organizational change are all intended to contribute to the same strategy. Moreover, they also use the same resources: staff capacity, money and management attention. Aside from sharing the same goal and resources, they also exchange requirements and opportunities for improvement. This works as follows. Based on day-to-day operation, opportunities for improvement are identified which can be taken up by procedures and systems for continuous improvement. This will ultimately result in successful implementation of the improvements. Day-to-day operation also provides requirements in cases of renewal, transformation or new business. These are taken up within the processes and systems of organizational change. This will ultimately result in the successful implementation of the organizational changes. If successful,

Table 5.1   The three types of operational processes

	RUN (the business)	CHANGE (the business)	
	Day-to-day operation	Continuous improvement	Organizational change
Ambition	Execution	Incremental improvement	Renewal/change/new business
Focus	Now	Tomorrow	Future
Organization	Line organization	Work streams	Program and projects
Governance	Hierarchy	Hierarchy, process and system owners	Change organization: steering committees, portfolio board, architecture board
Competencies	All competencies related to the type of services and support processes	Enterprise architecture, specifying, realizing, implementing	Change management, BTF, enterprise architecture, business transformation portfolio management, program and project management, business design (specifying), realizing, implementing
Level	Procedures	Processes	Entire organization/chain processes
Commonly used terms	Lights on, going concern, primary process, bottom-line results, operational processes	Business Process Management, Lean, Six Sigma, BiSL, Release Management	BTF, programs/projects, implementation, change management, transformations
Examples of issues	Absence due to illness, system faults, other errors, complaints	Inefficiency, constraints, untapped potential	Ambitions, innovation, renewal

both improvements and organizational changes result in performance gains, which must be incorporated into the budgets, forecasts and objectives for day-to-day operations. Continuous change and organizational change also exhibit interrelationships. When defining a change, we also identify opportunities for improvement that do not need to be handled in projects, but instead can be resolved in the continuous improvement procedures and systems. In the previous chapters, we have referred to these improvements as 'activities of the line organization' or 'change activities that are handed over to the responsible management'. However, these opportunities for improvement are also preconditions for realization of the intended business case and are, therefore, monitored as part of the organizational change.

The business transformation plan, as engineered, is an essential document for aligning day-to-day operations, process improvement and organizational change. The plan translates the strategy into the organizational changes needed to carry it out. In this process, we identify the investments, costs and capacity needed to implement the changes. The pace, level of ambition, organizational maturity and project risks are the main factors determining how much management attention is required.

In addition, the business transformation plan also defines the activities allocated to the line organization. Any activities that are preconditions for implementing the change are monitored as part of the business transformation (organizational change process). Some other action items that arise during the business transformation planning are passed to process improvement for further action. The same applies here as for the activities of the

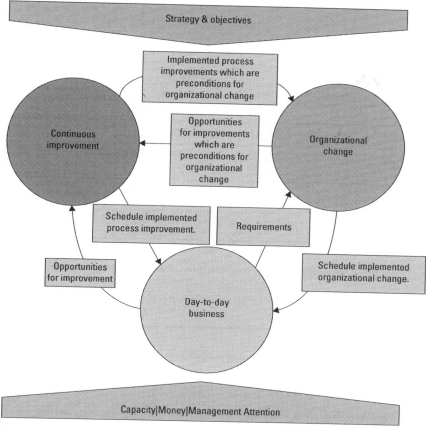

Figure 5.6   Interrelationships between day-to-day operation, continuous process improvement and organizational change

line organization. If relevant to the change, progress will be monitored. In the following subsections, we discuss the interfaces between day-to-day operation, process improvement and organizational change as shown in Figure 5.6.

5.2.1   Day-to-day operation, process improvement and organizational change contribute to the same strategy

An organization has just one overall strategy. All functional strategies such as the marketing strategy, IT strategy, etc., are actually derived from this – or at least they should be. Therefore, day-to-day operation, process improvement and organizational change are intended to achieve the same strategy. However, they do this in different ways.

Day-to-day operation is responsible for what are known as 'bottom-line results'. This means: provision of products and services with predefined performance requirements in areas such as delivery time and cost-price quality, resulting in satisfied customers and, hopefully, good revenues. The level of performance that is feasible for day-to-day operations is limited by the current design and implementation of the different aspects of running an organization

(Customers & Services, Processes & Organization, Information & Applications and IT Infrastructure & Facilities).

In contrast, continuous improvement and (structural) organizational change are specifically designed to improve the performance of day-to-day operations or ensure continuity by implementing improvements, renewals, expansions or replacements in one or more of the aspects of running an organization. Simply put: continuous improvement and organizational change ensure that day-to-day operations are at least just as able to deliver everything needed to carry out the strategy in terms of products, services and performance.

Figure 5.7 shows a simplified management cycle with the relevant connections. The same strategy is used to make plans for day-to-day operations, process improvement and organizational change. The bottom of the figure shows the execution of the different types of operations. As we will explain further on in this chapter, these operations are interrelated, which means they must be evaluated and learned as an integral whole.

Periodic evaluation, adjustment and alignment of both the business transformation plan *and* the annual plans comprise an effective management tool for the organization. An organization's planning cycle is crucial here. Typically, we see an annual planning process that defines the strategy and objectives before developing these into the business transformation plan and annual plans for the planning period. (See Figure 5.7.)

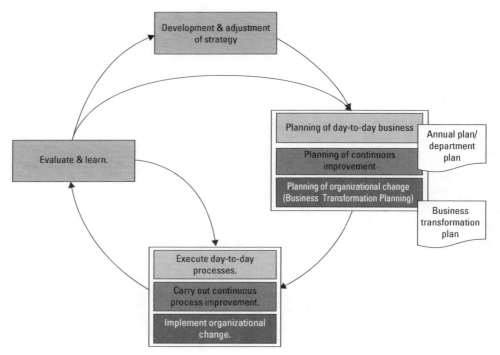

Figure 5.7   Simplified management cycle

During the planning period, we monitor progress at the different levels. Work is performed to apply changes in different parts of the organization. During and after the change, we monitor whether the desired change is also actually happening.

5.2.2   Day-to-day operations, process improvement and business transformation all deplete the same resources

If we ask an organization how it is organized, we are usually shown the well-known hierarchical chart. This traditional hierarchy primarily indicates how its day-to-day operations are organized. See Figure 5.8.

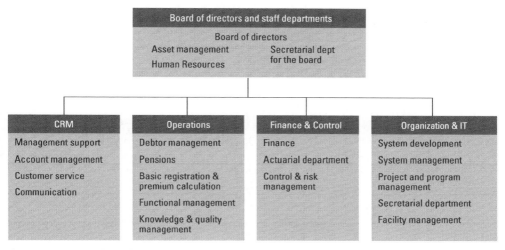

Figure 5.8   Example of hierarchical organizational structure of a Pension Insurance Provider

What is often less visible, is how process improvement is organized or how the change organization works. This is difficult because it would mean including more dimensions in the same diagram, with some employees appearing in more than one place. This is because process improvement and organizational change are not possible without the involvement of people from day-to-day operations – including management. We must make choices regarding the degree of involvement and the capacity that is desired and feasible. Management is part of the change organization in its role as executive, delegated executive, sponsor or steering committee member. Employees often participate in project teams to draft requirements and specifications and to test or implement changes. Therefore, the time available from management and employees in the organization must be divided between day-to-day operations, process improvement and organizational change. It is only through the full-time roles in the change organization, such as project leaders, marketeers, HR managers, business analysts, project communications specialists, etc., that the organization can maintain a flexible outer shell, with the hiring of external workers if necessary.

Integrated resource planning is often allocated to the business transformation portfolio management role. Integrated resource planning is necessary because we always need some of the same people for both the 'run' and the 'change'. The business transformation plan describes the capacity needed for a particular change. Naturally, the board of directors and management can still manage the organization based on the level of ambition and pace of change, or can increase capacity, such as by hiring outside staff. Annual plans and/or department plans provide information on the resources needed for day-to-day operations and for continuous improvement.

A similar state of affairs applies to the budget. The financial means available are generated by the day-to-day operations, at least in a healthy organization. Some of the cash flow or capital can be used for investments. Capital can also be drawn off for business transformation. The investment capacity is therefore dependent on the cash flow, the available capital and willingness to invest on the part of the board of directors and senior management. Budgets that are allocated to process- and system owners for continuous improvement cannot be used to implement organizational changes, and vice versa. For financial resources as well, we have a dependency between day-to-day operation, process improvement and structural organizational change. The business transformation plan describes the financial resources needed for change. Once again, the board of directors and the management can manage the organization based on the level of ambition and pace. Annual plans and/or department plans provide information on the resources needed for day-to-day operations and for continuous improvement.

The final shared resource to discuss here is management attention. Management attention is absolutely vital for a successful business transformation project. Yet the relevant managers and directors usually have packed schedules, and it can take weeks to get a meeting. We do not intend this as a complaint, because there are undoubtedly many other important or urgent matters that require management attention. We only want to highlight the fact that management attention is a scarce commodity in many organizations, and that we must explicitly take this into account when considering the level of ambition and pace of the organizational change. In any case, the business transformation plan outlines the amount of management attention required for the roles of project owner, stakeholder, steering committee member and sponsor.

5.2.3 Process improvement and organizational change are intended to optimize day-to-day operation

As mentioned above, process improvement and (structural) organizational change are intended to improve the performance of day-to-day operations or ensure continuity by implementing improvements, renewals or replacements in one or more of the aspects of running a business. Naturally, the preparation of business cases is also based on this principle. This process weighs the necessary investments against ensuring continuity, implementing cost reductions or achieving performance gains in day-to-day operations. This involves a major dependency. The investments made in process improvement and organizational change must be earned back in the day-to-day operations. Therefore, when making operational plans, it is only sensible to take into account increasing performance, higher sales or lower costs once any process improvements or organizational changes are implemented. Figure 5.9 clearly shows this. The same organizational strategy is used to make plans for day-to-day operations, process improvement and the business transformation plan for organizational change.

In this book, we will not go into further detail on what the plans for day-to-day operations and process improvement look like. In most cases, however, it is part of the regular planning cycle found in almost every organization. This often involves annual plans, sometimes supplemented with one or more long-term plans and functional plans.

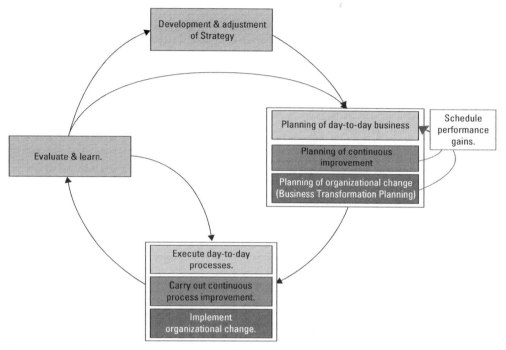

Figure 5.9   Simplified view of the management system (Kaplan & Norton, 2008)

Improvements, upgrades and replacements in the aspects of running a business must be factored in to the plans for day-to-day operation. In other words, the changes must measurably result in performance gains, as indicated in the business case, and this must be expressed in the plans for day-to-day operations.

The plans provide direction for the three types of operations shown in Figure 5.9. Overall evaluations are conducted to provide new knowledge. Here, we also check whether the improvements from the business case that were scheduled in the operational plans have actually been achieved. This may result in the refinement of the strategy or the various plans, or in adjustments to the operations.

5.3   Summary

In this chapter we have explained how to use the business transformation plan created with the BTF as a management tool for implementing the business transformation. We must always distinguish between two clear objectives for use. First, the business transformation plan is the basis for all competencies needed to implement structural organizational change, also known as change operations. The business transformation plan is the basis for the enterprise target architecture. This is the main deliverable for the enterprise architecture function. An existing enterprise target architecture provides vital input when preparing a business transformation plan. In addition to this, the business transformation plan provides the initial or adjusted business transformation portfolio, which the portfolio management role can use to manage the business transformation based on optimal added-value and customized allocation of resources. Changes are implemented by using the following competencies: program and project management, specification and implementation.

The second objective for use of the business transformation plan is to align day-to-day operations with process improvement and structural organizational change. Alignment between these three types of operations is necessary because they are each intended to contribute to the same strategy, using the same resources. Specifically, we are referring to capacity, money and management attention. Finally, we have a dependency related to the exchange of requirements and results, as well as factoring performance gains into the plans for day-to-day operations. These activities are coordinated by means of business transformation portfolio management.

6 Getting Started with the BTF!

In the preceding chapters, we explained what the BTF is. We have shown how to use the BTF to align the strategy and the objectives, and how the BTF can help us align the various aspects of running an organization. Next, we went through the planning process for the BTF: from the initiation phase to the development phase, ending with the delivery phase. In chapter 5 we focused on using a business transformation plan to shape and steer an organizational change. In this final chapter, we offer some additional practical tips for getting started with a business transformation plan.

Section 6.1 goes into detail on the question of how to use an all-encompassing framework like the BTF in a practical way. Next, in section 6.2, we provide a tool for testing whether the organization is ready for business transformation planning. In section 6.3, we discuss the management of expectations for a BTF project. Ambition is good, but we need to remain realistic. In section 6.4, we will describe how to use the BTF to create the business transformation plan. In section 6.5, we explain the main roles in the BTF. Finally, in section 6.6, we offer several tips that will help new business transformation planners to get started.

6.1 Use the BTF in a practical way that fits with the organization

After reading this book, we imagine that the reader may have gained the impression that the BTF is an incredibly extensive approach for turning the business strategy into a concrete business transformation portfolio. You may be wondering whether:
- It is necessary to go through all the steps of the entire framework;
- It will take too much time to carry out a BTF project.

The answer to the first question is 'yes', you must go through all of the steps. However, it does not always have to be all-encompassing, so it does not need to take an excessive amount of time. The purpose of going through all the steps of the entire framework is, on the one hand, to prevent a project from being defined too quickly without a clear idea of what it should accomplish, its interrelationships with other projects, its demarcations, etc. On the other hand, going through all the steps of the entire framework also ensures that all aspects of organizational design – with their interrelationships – are included in the implementation of the business transformation portfolio.

However, this doesn't mean that all aspects in the framework are equally important in every situation. During the initiation phase, we determine the purpose and the scope of the business transformation plan. The purpose and the scope are significant factors in determining the focus when creating the business transformation plan. If the business transformation plan is intended to resolve existing issues in the application landscape and develop the application landscape based on future-proof solutions and technologies, then obviously the focus will mainly lie on elaborating the aspects of Information & Applications and Infrastructure &

Facilities. However, in this case, it is still a good idea to examine the aspects of Customers & Services and Processes & Organization, just less extensively and in not so much detail. After all, changes in applications and infrastructure may also have consequences for processes, employees and customers.

The answer to the second question is 'no', there is not always a lot of time required to create a business transformation plan. Firstly, it is not the intention for the project team to disappear for months and later reappear again triumphantly with a business transformation plan. Instead, a business transformation plan is created in an iterative manner. You can deliver an initial version of a business transformation plan after just a few workshops. In this process, it is vital to touch on all of the aspects in the framework. It is much less important for all aspects to be completely worked out in detail: this can be handled in subsequent iterations. After every iteration we can determine where the focus of the next iteration should lie. This procedure fits in much better with 'agile' approaches, which have become increasingly popular in recent years.

Secondly, elaborating the details simply takes longer in certain cases. This depends not only on the desired level of detail, but also and especially on the availability of relevant documentation and knowledge. Almost all organizations have already examined many issues and already have various documents with proposals, approaches to solutions, constraint analyses, architectures, etc. Whether these documents are final versions or drafts is less important than whether the contents of the documents are of high quality and usable. If a lot of useful documents are already available for the aspects in the framework, then we can reuse these, which means of course that it will take much less time to elaborate further details than if no input at all were available. By making maximum use of what is already available, we can drastically reduce the BTF project lead times. However, the intention is not to use everything without question: it is important that all input is evaluated and integrated. For this reason, the availability and quality of useful documents are assessed in the initiation phase.

6.2   Use the initiation phase to test if the organization is ready for a BTF project

Before the actual start of a BTF project, it is a wise to get an idea of its usefulness and the likelihood of success within the organization. The assessment below will help you make the benefits and feasibility of the BTF transparent for your organization. First, score all questions. The far left means that the statement is completely correct; the far right means that it is completely incorrect. Next, add up the scores from blocks 1 and 2 and plot the result in the BTF readiness matrix (see Figure 6.1).

Table 6.1 Block 1: Benefits of business transformation planning for the business

Question	Completely correct				Completely incorrect
Strategic framework					
1	We have a clear mission, vision and strategy that are excellent tools for distinguishing ourselves.	3	3	4	5	5
2	We use performance indicators to steer ourselves in order to achieve strategic objectives.	1	2	3	4	5
Products & services					
3	Our industry is undergoing a major change. Customer needs are changing, new competitors are emerging and the supply market is regrouping.	1	2	3	4	5
4	We are a highly customer-oriented organization. We are proactive in marketing strategy, sales and service and we process customer contacts quickly and effectively. We have the right customer information.	1	2	3	4	5
5	We have a short time-to-market for introducing new products/ services or adjusting existing products/services (e.g. due to the impact of new legislation).	1	2	3	4	5
Processes					
6	Our administrative processes/systems are designed entirely around operational excellence (efficiency, low processing costs, short delivery times).	1	2	3	4	5
7	Running our organization (processes, culture, supply chain management, organizational structure) is now so complex and diverse that no one can really oversee everything. If we change one thing, it always has repercussions somewhere else, resulting in surprises.	5	4	3	2	1
Data and information systems					
8	Information and IT are absolutely vital to our organization.	5	4	3	2	1
9	Our information systems are of very high quality. Our systems meet the highest of quality standards and modern architecture principles, both functionally and technically.	1	2	3	4	5
10	Our data and information systems (number and complexity of applications, legacy systems, spreadsheets to support essential capabilities, data recording) have become so complex that no one can really oversee everything. If we change one thing, it always has repercussions somewhere else, resulting in surprises.	5	4	3	2	1
IT infrastructure					
11	We do not have a clear enough picture of which innovative developments there are in the IT supply market and how we can take advantage of these in the future.	5	4	3	2	1
Business transformation portfolio					
12	We have a clear business transformation portfolio, aligned with our business strategy and tested for feasibility.	1	2	3	4	5
Total score					

Table 6.2   Block 2: Feasibility of business transformation planning

Question		Completely correct				Completely incorrect
1	We have a clear business strategy. The management knows where they want to go and how to achieve the set goals.	5	4	3	2	1
2	It is not in our DNA to make long-term plans. Our management prefer to penetrate the market instead of wasting time drafting up plans for the future.	1	2	3	4	5
3	We see business transformation planning as something we have to do ourselves. You cannot and should not outsource it.	5	4	3	2	1
4	We have adequate capacity and quality available to develop business transformation plans. Both from business and from the IM/IT column.	5	4	3	2	1
5	We have a base of support in all levels of the organization to develop business transformation plans.	5	4	3	2	1
6	We have high quality input material for developing a business transformation plan. We have process and information architectures. And we have proper insight into the existing data and information systems (application portfolio).	5	4	3	2	1
7	Decision-making is well organized in our organization. We are decisive, we do this in general terms, not in detail, and we make bold choices.	5	4	3	2	1
Total score						

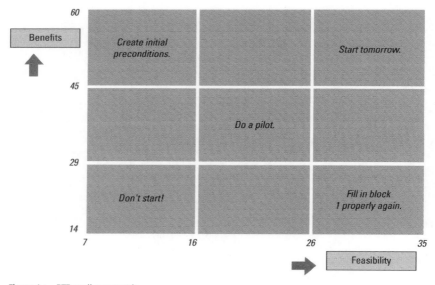

Figure 6.1   BTF readiness matrix

Of course, this assessment is only intended to provide an indication. The results are primarily used for critical consideration of the results: what conclusions can be drawn and what do they mean for the implementation of a BTF project within the organization?

Discuss the outcomes with different people in the organization. Do they see things the same way? Is there a base of support for the idea? If the assessment shows that there are benefits to be gained through business transformation planning, but feasibility is low, then it would be wise to firstly take action in order to develop the required disciplines and meet other preconditions. Some examples of other preconditions include: available capacity and budget, required amount of management attention, elaborating the strategy, the base of support among employees, etc.

6.3   The expectations of the business transformation plan have to be realistic

Once the most basic preconditions, a base of support and in-house capacity for business transformation planning are in place, we can begin. But where should we start, and what should we expect?

As noted in chapter 4, we always start with an initiation phase. In the initiation phase, we investigate and define the why, the what and the how of business transformation planning. It is important, if there are doubts about the feasibility of the BTF (see the assessment in the preceding section), that a great deal of attention is given to the objective and level of ambition in the initiation phase. However, an organization that does not, as yet, have much experience working with planning, architecture or controlling a business transformation portfolio can still successfully implement the BTF and reap benefits. In this case, we must ensure that the necessary disciplines are available for this, or that they can be sourced externally.

The expectations for using the BTF must be realistic. The quality of the final plan and what will happen in reality are also dependent upon how mature the organization already is in areas such as:
- Strategy and objectives;
- Strategic planning and control;
- Insight into and control over resources (time and money);
- Available product, process and information architectures;
- Capacity and quality of project management;
- Degree to which business transformation portfolio management has already been set up.

The BTF project must be appropriate for the maturity level of the organization. This does not mean that the business transformation plan should not be ambitious or aim to take the organization to the next level: it may even be necessary to 'stimulate the organization' in order to make the business transformation plan successful. However, it does mean that getting too far ahead of yourself is usually not such as good idea.

6.4   Use the BTF for structure and guidance in the business transformation plan

The BTF is also excellently suited to assist in structuring the final business transformation plan. Table 6.3 provides an initial approach for structuring a business transformation plan, but this is certainly not a complete picture.

Table 6.3   BTF checklist

Chapter	Topics
Introduction	Situation outline and motivation Objectives Choices and demarcation Approach Brief explanation of the BTF (so the plan can be read by people who have not been involved)
Strategy and Objectives	Mission/vision Environment analysis SWOT Strategy CSFs Objectives
Customers & Services	Guiding principles Analysis of current situation: • Products and services • Customers and customer roles • Distribution channels and media Outline of target situation Action items
Processes & Organization	Guiding principles Analysis of current situation: • Processes and/or capabilities • Organization and governance Outline of target situation Action items
Information & Applications	Guiding principles Analysis of current situation: • Information model • (Logical) information systems architecture • Current application landscape Outline of target situation Action items
IT Infrastructure & Facilities	Guiding principles Analysis of current situation: • Hardware and operating systems • Network and communication products • Database management systems • Professional programming tools • Tools for end users • Sourcing Outline of target situation Action items
Business transformation portfolio	Guiding principles • Cluster action items into candidate projects • Project charters and operational activities • Value/risk consideration and matrix • Planning for time, money and capacity

A fully developed business transformation plan is not suitable as an effective tool for communication with management and the board of directors. For this, we must prepare a separate document that sets out the main findings, conclusions and recommendations along with their interrelationships. We can do this in the form of a management presentation or a memo that consists of no more than four sheets of A4 paper. Please note: this is not a summary, but a separate document written specifically for the management and board of directors and with a clear goal. This often includes a request for specific decisions to be taken.

In addition to this, it is often a good idea to make a short presentation that is understandable for all employees in the organization, explaining the main findings, conclusions and results of the business transformation planning in an accessible way. The purpose of this is to actively inform all stakeholders in the organization.

6.5   All of the different stakeholders have their own role during business transformation planning

Business transformation planning involves a large number of people in an organization. However, certain people have more encompassing roles than others. This section gives a brief description of the main roles in business transformation planning. For each role, we indicate who will normally fulfill it, the corresponding tasks and responsibilities, the competencies required and the main do's and don'ts.

Executive
<u>Who:</u> Director or manager, such as the COO, CIO, change director, IT manager or business development manager.

<u>Tasks, responsibilities and authorizations regarding business transformation planning:</u>
- Can start and stop the project and grant discharge to the core team after completion;
- Ensures commitment from the management;
- Determines the assignment and objectives for the business transformation planning and bears final responsibility for the result;
- Provides resources, budget and capacity for implementation of the BTF;
- Ensures that the preconditions are fully satisfied so that the team can do its work properly;
- Ensures that decisions are made within a reasonable period of time during escalations.

<u>Competencies that (s)he brings to the table:</u>
- Strategic/tactical level, has a clear vision;
- Can make or effectively delegate decisions.

Do's and don'ts:
- Do - give people the freedom to help brainstorm new ideas and make maximum use of ideas and insights in the organization;
- Do - actively support the BTF, inspire fellow directors and managers with enthusiasm;
- Don't - use the business transformation plan as justification for a pre-defined outcome.

Project leader or 'lead consultant'

Who: Internal or external adviser, typically with a background in business administration.

Tasks, responsibilities and authorizations regarding business transformation planning:
- Bears responsibility for implementation of the BTF;
- Advises the management and board of directors;
- Ensures a carefully designed process;
- Supervises various work streams and interim results;
- Ensures consistency of the final plan;
- Facilitates decision-making in matters such as project prioritization.

Competencies that (s)he brings to the table:
- Is a trustworthy advisor for the board of directors and management;
- Is a good project leader. (S)he thoroughly understands that creating a business transformation plan is not an implementation project: it has all of the characteristics of an expedition. (S)he can handle this well;
- Has effective human factor skills and is able to put together a good team and guide complex interactions;
- Is an all-round expert in the field of business administration. (S)he can talk easily with all employees and departments about content, but also and especially make connections that others cannot see because they do not have a holistic overview;
- Can adequately participate in creative thinking regarding all aspects of running an organization and at every level: strategy, design and the business transformation portfolio.

Do's and don'ts:
- Do - use time as a resource (timeboxing);
- Do - communicate and keep everyone involved;
- Do - ensure that choices are made by the right people and at the right time;
- Don't - write the contents of the plan yourself;
- Don't - get too far ahead of yourself, both in terms of content and other factors, such as the speed of the project.

Portfolio manager

Who: Business transformation portfolio manager, project portfolio manager, manager or team leader within Project Management Office

<u>Tasks, responsibilities and authorizations regarding business transformation planning:</u>
- Ensures feasible business transformation portfolio and planning;
- Ensures that the projects can be included in the portfolio, i.e. that they are SMART enough;
- Provides templates for project charters, planning, prioritization, etc.;
- Ensures that the projects and activities have been included in the overall portfolio and that they can be properly controlled;
- Assesses project plans and portfolios for feasibility;
- Supports decision-making and prioritization of projects;
- Establishes the business transformation portfolio into regular procedures for business transformation portfolio management;
- Ensures that, after delivery of the business transformation plan, the decision makers can immediately proceed and a plan is already in place to provide the right resources so the project does not stall after delivery and the organization can start delivering the plans immediately.

<u>Competencies that (s)he brings to the table:</u>
- Knows what needs to happen to implement the plan in reality;
- Makes the necessary preparations for including the projects in the business transformation portfolio;
- Has extensive experience in stakeholder management;
- Keeps a focus on making the benefits tangible (instead of only focusing on costs).

<u>Do's and don'ts:</u>
- Do - use a project prioritization method that is highly detailed and as objective as possible;
- Do - use the key figures from previous projects to assess whether the estimates are realistic;
- Don't - set up a separate BTF portfolio but control all change activities in an integrated manner.

Subject-matter expert
<u>Who:</u> An employee from the organization with a great deal of knowledge in certain business processes or a certain discipline (department), such as Sales, Marketing, Operations, IT or Finance. A business transformation planning project team consists of multiple subject-matter experts.

<u>Tasks, responsibilities and authorizations regarding business transformation planning:</u>
- Brings specific expertise to the project team;
- Identifies existing constraints and opportunities;
- Details specific issues or conduct analyses;
- Assesses the detailed architectures for all dimensions in the BTF;
- Determines which action items are necessary to get from the current situation to the target situation;
- Coordinates with colleagues on approaches to solutions, on constraints and on action items.

Competencies that (s)he brings to the table:
- Knows the day-to-day business from personal experience.
- Can summarize how things are currently done because (s)he understands what is truly important and can participate in creative thinking at a certain conceptual level.

Do's and don'ts:
- Do - organize multiple consultations with your own peers and subordinates;
- Do - think in terms of opportunities rather than barriers;
- Do - avoid making judgments on other departments or disciplines and try to understand each other.

'Business/information analyst or architect'

Who: Internal or external analyst or architect.

Tasks, responsibilities and authorizations regarding business transformation planning:
- Contributes relevant (architecture) models, guidelines and guiding principles;
- Drafts and/or helps to draft the relevant (architecture) models and guiding principles;
- Indicates where constraints can be found in the organization;
- Conducts analyses or helps to answer research questions;
- Ensures cohesion between the different columns of the BTF;
- Ensures coordination with the architecture function;
- Following completion of the business transformation plan, bears full or partial responsibility for ensuring proper use and management of the architectures and guiding principles.

Competencies that (s)he brings to the table:
- Is used to thinking in terms of, and working with, architectures and guiding principles;
- Has a good overview of the products and services, the processes, the application landscape, data management and data flows;
- Is used to thinking in terms of trade-offs and different scenarios;
- Is used to conducting gap analyses;
- Has extensive knowledge on the origins of the application landscape;
- Makes preparations for maintaining the architectures and guiding principles;
- Serves as the liaison with other architects.

Do's and don'ts
- Do - introduce relevant models and guiding principles;
- Do - keep an eye on interrelationships;
- Do - identify the current applications and IT components, including associated costs;
- Do - help draft models and guiding principles and provide support in conducting analyses;
- Do - identify why choices were made in the past, but do not remain bound by these.

6.6 Successful application of the BTF requires a focus on the quality of the process, contents and use

The BTF is only successful if it produces a result, such as starting up important projects, making adjustments to projects that have already commenced, providing an improved method for the prioritization of projects, or establishing a clear foundation for the use of the plan in management cycles and line organization roles within the organization. A business transformation plan will only achieve results (and thus also success) if quality is guaranteed in three areas:
- Quality of the business transformation plan creation process;
- Quality of the contents of the business transformation plan;
- Quality in the use of the business transformation plan as a steering tool.

6.6.1 Quality of the creation process

The quality of the creation process is largely dependent upon the degree to which the use of the BTF has been aligned with the organization's goals and possibilities, the involvement and support of stakeholders and the lead time. Engineering a business transformation plan is not a goal in itself: it meets a specific need. This need often arises when the dynamics and complexity of the organization suddenly increase due to one or more factors. Once this happens, the organization recognizes the need to create a holistic overview and cohesion, and use these to redefine the plan for the next few years. The BTF helps in this process.

Business transformation planning starts with specific and realistic goals in which the management strongly believes.
The management must strongly support the objectives of the business transformation planning in order to ensure adequate attention and priority. Agreement with, and support from, the management are essential (e.g. Stoop & Silvius, 2013; Ward & Peppard, 2002). In order to establish the real underlying reason(s) and the key objectives, we need to choose a critical approach and ask the right questions. In addition, by basing the business transformation plan and the approach on the actual underlying reasons and objectives, the management and organization can recognize themselves in it, increasing the chances of getting it off the ground.

What should you do?
1. Find out how things work. Who plays what role, who has influence over what and what are their different values?
2. Interview all key stakeholders to get to know their values. Ask about their expectations and establish the specific underlying reasons and goals for the business transformation plan with them.

3. In the interviews, do not assume that everyone is familiar with the BTF. Provide a thorough explanation.
4. Ask follow-up questions. Do not necessarily be satisfied with quick answers. Use the 3Ws model: Why? Why? Why?
5. In the interviews, try to pin down the source of current resistance by asking about reasons for NOT using the BTF.
6. Use interview results and quotes when making the action plan for business transformation planning.
7. Have the action plan approved by the executive and reviewed by all stakeholders.
8. Ensure the proper provision of data and information to the business transformation planning project team.

The BTF is the start of an organizational change process involving the entire organization.
The base of support amongst the management who are present at the start of the business transformation planning should be maintained and, if possible, expanded during the project. This means first and foremost that we need a base of support from the management of all disciplines involved, such as: Marketing, Sales, Production, Financial Management, Communications and IT (e.g. Ward & Peppard, 2002). In addition to this, we must also mobilize and involve subject-matter experts for all of these disciplines. The business transformation plan must be the result of a process that the project team goes through, in conjunction with all stakeholders from all business disciplines involved. This ensures close cooperation between the different business disciplines *during* the business transformation planning, rather than only afterwards. This results in a better understanding of everyone's perspectives and values and the interrelationships between these (alignment). So the result is not just the business transformation plan itself, but more importantly the base of support from all stakeholders and thus also the energy and momentum to move forward with the planned change.

What should you do?
1. Determine the expertise needed in terms of content and the departments 'affected' by business transformation planning.
2. Form a small core team with the necessary content-related expertise and the authority to make design choices.
3. Make explicit agreements with the members of the core team on aligning the contents with colleagues and management. This means that it is not enough just to attend workshops! Ensure that the core team has enough time to arrange this alignment properly.
4. Ensure thorough support and guidance for the project team. A project leader and an experienced organization consultant serving as a facilitator and subject matter catalyst are indispensable.
5. Set up a focus group at the management level and task this group with creating a base of support in the different departments that are impacted by the business transformation plan.
6. Draft a communications plan for the business transformation planning: who is informed of what, when and in what way.

7. Ensure regular coordination with management on important interim results so the decision-making process does not result in any surprises (pre-cook).

Business transformation planning does not last much longer than three months!
One of the first questions to answer is how much time do we need for business transformation planning. Experience has shown that a lead time of three months is 'an optimal timeframe'. The lead time cannot be much shorter than this because you need the time to sort out the complexity. We have to do a reasonable amount of investigation and analysis and share the overviews, ideas and decisions with numerous stakeholders. Moreover, business must continue as usual during a business transformation planning, which means stakeholders cannot be 100% available.

However, the lead time should not be much longer than this either. Management needs the holistic overview and essential design choices in the business transformation plan today, rather than tomorrow, in order to give proper direction in resolving day-to-day problems and issues. In addition to this, a limited lead time also ensures that the stakeholders have to restrict themselves to the essentials and that they cannot waste too much time discussing the details. A limited lead time also helps to maintain momentum and free up key individuals.

A limited lead time requires time boxing and making choices regarding scope. For optimal use of the time available, it is recommended that you start working with short cycles and prepare and prefill as much as possible based on pre-existing documentation. Working with brief iterations allows reconsideration of choices made in the past in relation to other choices. It is not possible or necessary to detail current issues, but it is certainly necessary to identify them as specifically and explicitly as possible so that they can be detailed further down the road, for example during preliminary studies. The business transformation plan is more of a development plan than a blueprint.

What should you do?

1. Make the scope very clear and explicit. What will we do and what will we not do, and to what level of detail?
2. Define time boxes and plan the workshops in advance. By doing so, the timelines are clear to everyone and the workshop planning keeps the pressure on. One example of a good schedule would be one weekly workshop with the core team and a further workshop every two or three weeks with the focus group.
3. Use the available documentation as much as possible. Don't go for a perfect model.
4. Work interactively in short cycles and ensure clear guidance to the core team, for example by starting every day with a brief meeting to distribute the work and checking the progress regularly throughout the day.
5. 'Park' discussions and turn these 'white spots' into action items in the business transformation plan so they can be examined further at a later stage.

6.6.2 Quality of the contents of the business transformation plan

The quality of the contents of the business transformation plan is primarily determined by the degree to which the complexity is made manageable: the contents must be understandable to all stakeholders, the essentials must be clear, as must be the characteristics and feasibility of the design choices.

The BTF requires a tool to manage the complexity!
Creating a business transformation plan involves a high degree of complexity that is often underestimated. In order to manage the complexity, it is necessary to split the plan up into manageable parts and obtain a clear understanding of the interrelationships between these parts. This means we must have a framework that helps to divide and monitor the complexity.

What should you do?

1. Use the BTF that encompasses both the organization and IT domains and that emphasizes ordering and structuring over completeness and formal modeling methods.
2. Determine the methods, visualization techniques and models already in use in the organization (standards) and establish whether they can be used within the framework.
3. Remind yourself and the core team that the framework or method is a tool, not a goal. Use frameworks/methods as checklists, not like a forms to be completed.
4. Explicitly monitor the interrelationships between the different business domains on the one hand and the strategy and action on the other hand.
5. Focus on one component of the framework at a time in order to gradually gain an insight into its complexity and how best to make it manageable.

A good business transformation plan should be in the 'language' of the stakeholders!
We can only achieve a base of support for, and involvement in, the business transformation plan amongst stakeholders, if the 'language' we use in the business transformation plan matches the conceptual framework and the frame of reference of those same stakeholders. After all, it is always easier to explain what you mean and what you want in a language that you have mastered! Often, each discipline has its own view of the organization and uses its own tools and models for analysis. For instance, marketeers think in terms of product/ market combinations, marketing mix and pricing models, whereas IT specialists think about system architectures and infrastructures. The BTF has the crucial task of integrating all of these worlds together so all stakeholders recognize their issues and understand how the proposed solutions resolve them. Of course, this places high demands on the project team: they must be able to communicate well with all stakeholders, preferably in the 'language' used in the world of these stakeholders.

What should you do?

1. Reuse pre-existing, accepted and recognizable models: do not introduce any new 'DIY' models unless necessary. Ensure recognition: every business and business domain has its own models.

2. Involve everyone in the brainstorming, even if the topic in question doesn't relate to the duties of some core team members. A marketeer's perspective on data and information systems, for instance, may be enlightening! In addition, this provides cross-pollination and acceptance for the solution.
3. Have members of the core team detail certain components themselves (but ensure clear steering and guidance).
4. Have members of the core team explain/present certain components of the business transformation plan themselves.

Stick to the essentials!
Highlighting the essentials means omitting minor details and using visualizations. Most managers are overwhelmed by information and reports and need a holistic overview and a clear path forward. Some professionals often laugh this off. They talk about making 'children's comics' or explaining things in 'mickey mouse' terms. However, these kindergarten references are completely misplaced: we have seen that business transformation plans consisting of a relatively small number of interrelated, specific and smart PowerPoint visualizations are much more effective and communicate much better than thick reports filled with text.

What should you do?
1. Visualize! A picture is still worth more than a thousand words.
2. Use PowerPoint slides instead of a text document: this forces you to provide the key information and omit excessive details.
3. For each slide, clearly indicate the essentials in the title.
4. Check regularly that the common thread is clear. Create interim versions of the business transformation plan regularly and discuss them thoroughly. For instance, we can put up the different slides on the wall of the project room and discuss them with the core team.

A business transformation plan should be abstract, but never vague!
A vague plan does not provide clear choices on the key issues. Vague plans result in sometimes endless discussions, varying interpretations and thus also in stagnation in the change process. The business transformation plan must be 100% clear with regard to when the different changes to the current situation are required and when they should be implemented in order to best achieve strategic objectives and the target situation.

What should you do?
1. Put together a core team with the authority and appropriate expertise, at the right level of abstraction (management level), and with management and other experience in the relevant business domain.
2. Never be satisfied with vague terminology and buzz words. Always ask follow-up questions!
3. If necessary, confront members of the core team about the vagueness of their statements.
4. Make the impact of design choices explicit. What will I be unable to do if I make this choice? What is needed to implement this design choice?

6.6.3 Quality of the usage of the business transformation plan

Even though the final version of the business transformation plan is complete and the project team has been discharged, the organization is still not quite ready. It is now up to management to use the business transformation plan for steering and monitoring programs and projects. Proper and active involvement of management should ensure that they become aware of this during business transformation planning.

Hurray, a business transformation plan! But the real work is only just about to commence!
The effective use of a business transformation plan as a steering tool is only possible through properly embedding it in the organization (e.g. Stoop & Silvius, 2013; Wagter et al. 2005). This means that responsibilities are assigned for the management, maintenance and monitoring of the plan and for monitoring its contents by a controlling architect. Typically, drafting and monitoring the program planning based on the business transformation plan and any associated decision-making on projects are allocated to a program manager. In addition to the allocation of these responsibilities, we must also pay attention to decision-making and reporting structures.

What should you do?
1. Identify the governance structure before starting business transformation planning and determine where any potential risks lie.
2. Make sure these risks can be discussed with the executive and identify possible solutions.
3. Involve the current program manager(s) and architects from the start of the business transformation planning so they start learning to work with it on day one.
4. Establish the business transformation portfolio in close collaboration with the managers who determine project priorities in practice (change boards, project boards, advisory boards, information management boards).
5. During completion, establish agreements with the executive on the allocation of responsibilities for the management and maintenance of the business transformation plan and for the management and maintenance of the business transformation portfolio. In addition, establish agreements on decision-making and reporting. In this process, use pre-existing governance structures wherever possible.

In our view, the BTF is not successful until the business transformation plan produces a result, such as making adjustments in projects that have already commenced, developing a better method of prioritizing projects or establishing the plan in the management cycles and line organization roles within the organization. This places demands not only on the quality of the content of the business transformation plan, but also on the process used in drafting it and the degree to which the organization is able to use the business transformation plan as a steering tool: E(ffectiveness) = Q(uality) × A(cceptance) × U(se). Only when all three of these requirements are met will the business transformation plan provide a solid foundation in today's complex and rapidly changing world. This will make the BTF a success!

Appendix 1 The Novius Business Empowerment framework and the other Novius frameworks

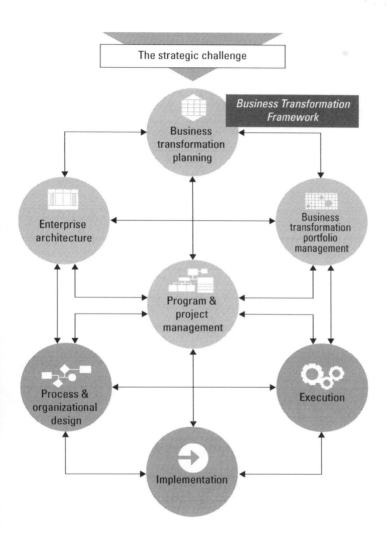

Literature

Aalst, W. Van der and K. Van der Hee, 2004. *Workflow Management: Models, Methods, and Systems.* The MIT Press

Bartunek, J. M. and M. K. Moch, 1987. 'First-Order, Second-Order, and Third-Order Change and Organization Development Interventions: A Cognitive Approach', in: The Journal of Applied Behavorial Science (NTL Institute)

Beijen, M., E. Broos and E. Lucas, 2003. *Business-informatieplanning, grip op organisatieverandering en ICT-inzet.* Kluwer

Blackwell, R.D., P.W. Miniard and J.F. Engel, 2001. *Consumer behavior, ninth edition.* South-Western College Pub

Boddy, D., A. Boonstra and G. Kennedy, 2009. *Managing Information systems: Strategy and organisation.* Prentice Hall

Caluwé, L. De, and H. Vermaak, 2003. *Learning to Change - A guide for organizational change agents.* Sage

Collins, J. and J. Porras, 1994. *Built to last: Successful habits of visionary companies.* Random House

Hamel, G. and C.K. Prahalad, 1996. *Competing for the future.* Harvard Business Review Press

Hatch, M.J., 1997. *Organization Theory, Modern, Symbolic, and Postmodern Perspectives.* Oxford University Press

Hinssen, P., 2011. *Business IT Fusion, Second Edition.* Lannoo Publishers

Johnson, G., K. Scholes and R. Whittington, 2002. *Exploring Corporate Strategy 6th ed.* FT/Prentice Hall

Kaplan, R.S. and D.P. Norton, 1993. Putting the Balanced Scorecard to work. In: Harvard Business Review, September - October. 1993

Kaplan, R.S. and D.P. Norton, 2004. *Strategy maps. Converting intangible assets into tangible outcomes.* Harvard Business School Publishing Corporation, Boston

Kaplan, R.S. and D.P. Norton, 2008. *Execution premium. Linking strategy to operations for competitive advantage.* Harvard Business School Publishing Corporation, Boston

Kennedy, D., 2013. *No B.S. Direct Marketing: The Ultimate No Holds Barred Kick Butt Take No Prisoners Direct Marketing for Non-Direct Marketing Businesses, 2nd edition.* Entrepreneur Press

Kim, W.C. and R. Mauborgne, 2004. *Blue Ocean Strategy.* HBS Press

Kotler, Ph. and G. Armstrong, 2012. *Principles of Marketing, 14th edition.* Pearson

Marcus, J., N. van Dam, N. and Methurst, K., 2007. *Organisation & Management: An International Approach.* Noordhoff Uitgevers

McAfee, A., 2006. Mastering The Three Worlds of Information Technology. In: Harvard Business Review, November 2006

Mintzberg, H., B. Ahlstrand and J.B. Lampel, 2002, 2008 (2nd revised edition). *Strategy Safari, The complete guide through the wilds of strategic management.* Prentice Hall

Mulders, M., 2014. *101 Management models.* Noordhoff

Office of Government Commerce, 2011. *Management of Portfolios,* TSO

Osterwalder, A. and Y. Pigneur, 2010. *Business Model Generation: A Handbook for Visionaries, Game Changers, and Challengers*. Wiley

Peelen, E. and R. Beltman, 2013. *Customer Relationship Management*. Pearson Education

Pettigrew, A. and R. Whipp, 1991. *Managing Change for Competitive Success*. Wiley-Blackwell

Pietersma, P., M. Van Assen and G. Van den Berg, 2009. *Key Management Models: The 60+ models every manager needs to know, Second Edition*. Prentice Hall.

Porter, M.E., 1980. *Competitive strategy: Techniques for analyzing industries and competitors*. The Free Press

Porter, M.E., 1985. *Competitive advantage: Creating and sustaining superior performance*. The Free Press

Porter, M.E., 1998. *The Competitive Advantage*. Simon & Schuster

Reinartz, W. J.S. Thomas and Kumar, 2005. Balancing Acquisition and Retention Resources to Maximize Customer Profitability. In: Journal of Marketing. January 2005, vol. 69, no. 1, pp. 63-79

Reinartz, W., J.S. Thomas and V. Kumar, 2005. Balancing Acquisition and Retention Resources to Maximize Customer Profitability. In: Journal of Marketing, vol. 69, January 2006, pp. 63-79

Rockart, J., 1979. Chief Executives Define Their Own Information Needs. In: Harvard Business Review, March/April 1979, pp. 81-92

Sinek, S., 2011. *Start with why*. Penguin Books Ltd.

Slack, N., S. Chambers and R. Johnston, 2010. *Operations management, sixth edition*. Pearson Education

Sorger, S., 2011. *Marketing Planning - Where Strategy Meets Action*. Abridged

Stoop, J. and G. Silvius, 2013. The relationship between the process of Strategic Information Systems Planning and its success; An explorative study. In: System Sciences (HICSS), 2013, 46th Hawaii International Conference

Ten Have, S., 2003. *Key Management Models: The Management Tools and Practices that will improve your business*. FT Press

The Open Group, 2013. *TOGAF 9.1 Specification*. Retrieved from https://www.opengroup.org/architecture/togaf91/downloads.htm

Treacy, M. and F. Wiersema, 1997. *The discipline of market leaders*. The Perseus Book Group

Wagter, R., M. Van den Berg, J. Luijpers, and M. Van Steenbergen, 2005. *Dynamic Enterprise Architecture: How to Make it Work*. Wiley

Ward, J. and J. Peppard, 2002. *Strategic planning for information systems, 3rd edition*. Wiley

Weske, M., 2012. *Business Process Management: Concepts, Languages, Architectures (Second Edition)*. Springer

Wilson, H., R. Street and L. Bruce, 2008. *The Multichannel Challenge, Integrating customer experiences for profit*. Elsevier/Butterworth-Heinemann

Index

17814184R00096

Printed in Great Britain
by Amazon